The Winning Trader

Developing a Mental Edge for Market Success

complete information on all financial instruments. Screens can be loaded with real time data from multiple sources or trimmed back to focus on essentials.

A Wide-Angle View

Using fast, reliable data from Townsend Analytics, RealTick lets individual and institutional traders track Nasdaq and listed stocks, futures, options, indices, currencies and foreign instruments. Traders can review current prices, historical performance, fundamental data and a wide range of technical indicators in a variety of charts, tables, tickers, depth of market displays, and more.

Direct Access

Market analysis and order entry are seamlessly integrated in RealTick. Use market information and analytics for decision support and simply click on a bid or ask to enter an order. RealTick also supports automated order entry through RealTick scripting. Link order-entry enabled windows to charts and quote screens for instant symbol changes. Send orders directly to markets such as Archipelago, NASDAQ, NYSE, Eurex, Xetra and Globex. RealTick supports the most basic to the most sophisticated orders from market and limit orders to reserve, discretionary, pegged and conditional orders.

Choices

Trading is about choices. RealTick has relationships with many direct access broker dealers. A RealTick subscriber who has an account with one of these broker dealers can trade directly from RealTick to any electronic market. A subscriber can also use RealTick for market information and trade through their broker of choice.

Take Control

RealTick gives traders the control and flexibility to determine the analysis tools that work best for their investment needs. Subscribers to RealTick are able to configure their screens to reflect their particular trading style and insight. This open interface and analysis provided by the technology coupled with controlling one's emotions in today's markets can lead to more effective trading decisions.

Discover the infinite opportunities of RealTick
For more information visit www.realtick.com

The Winning Trader

Developing a Mental Edge for Market Success

Michael S. Shopshire, Ph.D.

Innerworth Press
Tarzana, CA

Published by StrahmColor and Innerworth Press, a division of Innerworth

Printed in the United States of America

Library of Congress Cataloging-in-Publication Data is available.

ISBN 0-9728095-0-3

The essence of boredom is to be found in obsessive search for novelty. Satisfaction lies in mindful repetition - the discovery of endless richness in subtle variations of familiar themes

-George Leonard

To the traders who have no need for glory

Table of Contents

Contributors

Most of the selections in this book were columns written by Dr. Shopshire for the Innerworth.com website and the *Mind Over Markets*™ newsletter. The following authors wrote additional articles.

Amy A. Zillian

All the pieces fit; Moving full speed ahead; Forward opportunities; You are brilliant; Exit formulas; Being out of there; Stop dependence; Roomy trading plans; Don't fight the markets, flow with it; What will they think?; If P, Then Q; Resistance and momentum.

Innerworth Staff Writers

A winning attitude; It's how you react; Do it yourself trading; Timely action; A totally open mind; A firm direction; Watch your confidence level; Don't get high on your success; What motivates your trading?; What drives you?; Get off the roller coaster; Planning for success; The value of stops; Professionalism means less emotion; An avalanche of anxiety; Fighting fear; How to deal with fear; Who's the better traders?; Envy reduces effectiveness; The will to get out; Recovering from a bad day; Losing found money.

Introduction

Many are drawn to trading, but few are chosen for success. If trading is so difficult, then why pursue it? Numerous reasons come to mind, but first and foremost is the personal and financial freedom that trading offers. Since the onset of the Industrial Revolution, people have sought refuge from the daily grind: commuting to work, working tirelessly to satisfy performance quotas, and struggling to find a balance between working productively and having enough leisure time to enjoy one's family and friends. Trading seems to offer a solution to many of the woes of modern times: traders set their own hours, are accountable only to themselves, and make a relatively great deal of income doing something they love. Unfortunately, success is elusive with the majority of those trying to succeed failing in the first six months.

Why is success so elusive? The major reason is that the markets are extremely hard to master. Financial scholars and applied economists have tried to predict the markets with little success. It's not simply a matter of identifying a set of key variables that predict market prices, and developing and implementing a foolproof trading strategy that will work indefinitely in market to market. The factors that underlie market dynamics are often unknown and unanticipated. In addition, markets are largely the result of mass psychology: That is, the attitudes and beliefs of traders and investors who are easily swayed by media accounts and a human emotional tendency to act on fears and avoid the regret of losses. As psychologists and behavioral economists argue, people trading the markets are often illogical or "irrational," and this makes the markets unpredictable, and thus, success hard to achieve. For example, the recent dot-com bubble illustrates how prices can be based more on the opinion of the masses rather than fundamental economic principles. The history of the markets is spotted with bubbles and bursts, which are largely the result of psychological processes.

Our common sense tells us that putting in time and effort leads to a reward, but not in the markets. One can work long hours as a trader and still end up breaking even or losing money as a result of his or her efforts. It takes a special kind of person to succeed in this kind of environment. One must be able to persist in an atmosphere of chaos and uncertainty; one must not be disappointed easily upon encountering failure, yet not be excessively elated or boastful upon achieving success, which may be transitory considering the ever-changing market conditions.

In this book, we have delineated the mindset, personality style, and decision-making processes of the winning trader. We've outlined the problems, both short- and long-term issues, along with situational, motivational, and personality factors, that predispose trading success. We also provide the mental and psychological strategies that traders can use to neutralize these problems.

Successful traders are hard to find. At Innerworth we conducted in-depth interviews with over 100 traders of some nototiety. Over a quarter ended in the waste basket, and of the rest that were published, the reality is that remarkably few were genuinely successful traders - the mantra for many was, "If you can't do, then teach or start a trading website." So many had made some quick money in the bull market, only to find that true trading success was a lot more elusive when the markets changed in 2000; it was easier to make a living selling services to novice traders.

What winning traders know, and what novice traders have trouble accepting, is that one's psychology plays an important role for trading success. At Innerworth, we argue that success is a matter of looking inward towards one's personal psychology to find the answers. Hopefully, you will see the value of this approach after reading this book.

A book on trading psychology isn't novel. Many books on investment psychology have been written in the past decade, but our book is innovative in that it is one of the few books that reflect a collaboration between psychologists and traders. Non-psychologists who seem to make up psychological theory as they go along write most investment psychology books. Such an approach may be interesting and useful, but in the final analysis, it is merely opinion and conjecture. An alternative approach is possible: one that combines experiences of successful traders with the scientific studies from the fields of clinical, personality, cognitive, and social psychology, and the new field of behavioral finance. A vast research literature has been compiled in these areas, and such information is useful to traders. Unfortunately, many scholars often write to communicate with each other; the original findings are presented in a complex manner, which is difficult to understand. At Innerworth, we have found pertinent academic articles and tried to communicate the main points to our readers in a straightforward manner. Our goal is to provide traders not only with conventional wisdom of professional traders, but with research findings they can use to improve their trading performance.

Overview

This book consists of a collection of essays originally published in the Innerworth *Mind Over Markets*™ newsletter or on Innerworth.com. Since the essays were originally stand-alone columns, you can start at any point in the book and read one essay at a time. You don't have to start from the beginning and read straight through, although the essays are arranged by topic areas, and later essays often build on ideas introduced in earlier essays. Look at this compendium as a reference book that addresses your own personal psychological issues. Read the book through, identify the issues that are pertinent to you, and earmark those essays for later reference. Then, you can return to those essays, and read them over and over to help you develop your mental edge.

The chapters in this book fall under three general themes: peak performance, unconscious motives and personality, and behavioral finance. Each perspective has something to offer, but some people may find they prefer one perspective over another.

Peak performance: Psychologists in many different areas, such as clinical, industrial, and sports psychology, study how humans function optimally in interpersonal and social settings. They try to help people achieve high levels of performance. Everyone can improve their performance regardless of their occupation. It's not that traders have "unconscious" psychological problems, according to peak performance psychologists. But they can benefit through carefully monitoring their investment behaviors and alleviating potential problems that may hinder their performance. For example, removing any possible hindrance, such as stress, interpersonal conflict, or poor moods, can improve one's performance. Everyone experiences these issues to some extent, and through self-awareness and specific cognitive-behavioral strategies, one can master these issues and prevent them from interfering with trading.

Unconscious motives and personality: Some, but not all, traders and investors may be guided by unconscious motives. Personality and unconscious motives may not have short-term consequences for some people, but for others, these factors predict long-term success. The trading literature is replete with traders who have achieved phenomenal success in the short-term, yet have failed in the end because they ignored and did not address more deep-seated underlying psychological dynamics. To some, the discussion of unconscious motives may seem like a lot of "psycho-babble" and "over-pathologizing." That's a good point. It's not the case that all traders have unconscious motives that act below the surface to influence trading behavior, but some do. It's useful to learn about what these unconscious motives might be. If you think it applies to you, then explore it further. If you think it doesn't apply to you, that's fine too.

Behavioral Finance: Many academic researchers in the field of finance now admit that the efficient market hypothesis is not valid. Behavioral economists have turned to psychology to explain why market prices fluctuate. Some have gone as far as saying, “It’s about 90% psychology.” Scholars in behavioral finance are interested in whether they can explain market prices by turning to well controlled experimental studies in cognitive and social psychology, which suggest that humans are overconfident, risk averse, and are irrational with it comes to making decisions. We present several essays that show how all traders are prone to decision-making biases and irrational thinking styles when making investment decisions.

Each chapter consists of essays that address one or more of these themes. The first chapter introduces the topic of investment psychology by drawing parallels between trading and everyday activities for which most people have a clear understanding. When trying to develop skills in new areas, it is useful to relate what one is trying to learn to what one already knows. Chapter 1 is a collection of essays that clarify trading through the use of analogies.

Developing the proper mental edge is a matter of developing the proper mindset: on the one hand, one needs to be confident and sure of oneself, but on the other hand, behavioral economists warn that traders and investors can be overconfident most of the time. The essays in Chapters 2 and 3 address finding a balance between extreme humility and overconfidence. Chapter 2 covers how one can develop a strong sense of self-esteem and self worth, along with developing a positive mindset that can help you keep yourself in the right frame of mind, so you are confident, carefree, and in the moment: ready to identify trading opportunities and capitalize on them. Chapter 3 covers various perspectives on overconfidence, along with ways that you can identify overconfidence and ensure that it does not adversely influence your trading.

Chapter 4 covers the unconscious motives that may undermine success and the personality traits that exemplify effective traders. Chapter 5 covers risk management, with particular emphasis on how managing risk can help you preserve not only your financial capital, but your psychological capital as well.

Chapters 6 and 7 address decision-making processes. Chapter 6 addresses how emotions can interfere with decisions: essays cover how a variety of emotions can impact your decision-making, and what you can do to control your emotions. Finally, Chapter 7 addresses the decision-making biases that all traders should be aware of and eliminate. Essays describe common decision-making biases along with current research studies that address these biases.

Chapter 1

Thinking In Terms of Analogies

When trying to develop skills in a new area, it is useful to relate what one is trying to learn to what one already knows; it is helpful to think in terms of analogies. When one uses an analogy, one infers that if two or more things are similar in some respects, they are similar in other respects. There is a very human tendency to equate previously learned skills with new skills one is trying to develop. It's easier to understand a new topic if it can be related to a topic that one already understands. This is especially true of trading. Trading the markets is difficult and it's easier to gain a clear understanding of it if we relate it to topics we already understand. The essays in this chapter clarify trading through the use of analogies.

Trading is similar to a plethora of activities: Trading is like playing sports, surfing, or driving a car; technical analysis is an art; traders are intuitive scientists, or amateur mathematicians. Although thinking in terms of analogies helps one understand trading, it's important to remember that one is merely using an analogy as a guide: Don't confuse the analogy with the actual phenomenon you are trying to understand. Trading can be similar to a particular activity, but it is also quite different. Let's review some common trading analogies and consider how they are similar to trading, but also dissimilar.

Scientist: A scientist develops hypotheses about general laws of nature, collects data, and tests the validity of these hypotheses. Traders similarly develop hypotheses about the markets. They try to gauge market sentiment, predict what the market will do, and test out the hypothesis by putting on a trade and seeing what happens. But scientists conduct studies to find basic laws that are repeatable. Scientists have tried to study the markets with little success. Unfortunately, the markets are too random and chaotic to find consistent support for general laws. It's important to remember that when making a trade. The markets are not as predictable as science requires, so it's not useful to pretend that one can make such predictions. Don't over-analyze and don't strive for predictability. Accept the fact that the markets are unpredictable.

Sports: Trading is a lot like playing sports. Professional athletes are rewarded for having extremely well-developed skills. Trading similarly requires well-developed skills. Traders practice, prepare, and get ready to "play" the markets when they see an opportunity. Trading is a lot like playing a sport, but it does require that one learn trading methods, which require relatively little physical activity compared to playing sports. And the markets are a little less predictable compared to what the other team or an opponent might do.

Artist: Art is often difficult to understand. Ever see modern art? It's hard to see what makes it art. But it is. It's all a matter of context. Looking at a chart pattern and interpreting a seemingly random pattern of lines as a trading opportunity is a skill that is similar to that of an artist appreciating the subtle nuances of a painting. When evaluating a chart in the right context, one can see and perceive a pattern that can lead to a big payoff. But trading isn't purely art. It's useful to have an artistic inclination, but artists can afford to let their art speak for itself. Traders need to be accurate in their interpretations of the market or they won't make a profit.

Merchant: It has often been said that traders should approach trading like a well-run business, such as a successful merchant. Merchants are very systematic when it comes to planning and maintaining an inventory, and selling merchandise. But merchants usually have a good idea of what the public needs. Supply and demand in terms of the markets are a little more complicated. Sometimes, fundamental forces of supply and demand have little to do with price movements, and it's important to remember that when trading.

In summary, analogies can be useful when trying to understand trading, but remember, an analogy is merely an analogy. Trading may appear similar to an activity you already understand, but remember it may also be very different. In the rest of this chapter, these analogies are explored in greater depth.

Trader as Scientist

Some traders see a parallel between trader and scientist: both study past trends, develop a clearly defined hypothesis, and test the hypothesis by collecting data and analyzing it. For example, consider the goal of a physicist who tries to predict the rate at which an object will fall to the ground. Objects of the same shape fall to the ground at the same rate, regardless of weight. Thus, if you know how far an object must fall, you can calculate how long it will take to hit the ground. The scientist tries to study laws that are repeatable, so that these laws can be used to make predictions. They also try to find exceptions to the rule. Friction is a variable that is the exception; a feather doesn't fall to the ground as fast as a sphere of the same weight. Knowing the exceptions improves prediction.

How is trading like science? Traders form hypotheses about market consistencies and try to gauge the reliability of these consistencies. Take the Elliott wave principle, for example. It's assumed that some stock and futures prices correspond to the Elliot Wave pattern. Working under this assumption, traders, who use this approach, try to find price action that matches this pattern in an effort to make predictions of future prices. They try to determine when the rule applies and when it does not. The Elliott Wave principle is a theory that guides the hypotheses the trader makes regarding the markets: It provides the basis for an educated guess. Once formulated, the trader collects data from the market and tests the hypothesis; he or she sees if the market action supports the hypothesis. Just like a scientist, seasoned traders approach the markets with a well-defined trading plan, and systematically determine whether the plan is supported. They do so objectively and rationally. They don't let their emotions get in the way of sound decision-making.

It's vital that traders act like scientists when approaching the markets, but it's equally important to remember that trading the markets is different from finding support for scientific principles. It's somewhat encouraging to believe that market patterns are recurring, and if only one can identify these patterns, one can make money. It makes trading seem less overwhelming and success easier to achieve. But it's also important to remember that trading is not science. Scientists have shown in the last two decades that there are no repeatable patterns in the markets. The markets are random, meaning that no mathematical or statistical models can be used to predict the market with an acceptable amount of accuracy. That's what makes trading so hard. Skillful trading is an art, rather than a science. Traders are what psychologists call "intuitive scientists" in that they test hypotheses about the markets in a scientific fashion, but fall short of using formal scientific methods to test and find support for their hypotheses.

Although analogies are interesting, thought provoking, and sometimes enlightening, an analogy is merely an analogy; it's not an exact depiction of reality. If it were, then it wouldn't be an analogy, would it? So in thinking of the markets, it is clarifying to remember that seasoned traders approach trading as an intuitive scientist, constantly formulating hypotheses and testing them out in a calm and objective manner. At the same time, however, remember that no one has found patterns in the markets that are as replicable as science requires. So don't get too carried away thinking the market is more predictable than it is. Analogies are enlightening if you look at both the similarities and differences.

Riding the Wave

Charles Dow, in an influential series of articles in the *Wall Street Journal*, proposed that prices move in waves. A bullish trend is established and everyone follows it. Some would say that the key is to identify whether the market is bullish or bearish, depending on one's timeframe, getting on the bandwagon, taking advantage of the trend, and making a profit. Of course, understanding and predicting the markets is not very easy, but it's sometimes useful to think of trading in this simple way. Some traders draw an analogy between surfing and trading. A surfer tries to find a wave that is high enough and moves with enough force to ride. One tries to ride the wave as far as possible, either reaching the shore or getting off before getting thrown off.

If you are new to the markets or have not been very successful, it's useful to try this simple trading approach. Look at indicators of momentum and try to determine whether the market is bearish or bullish. If it's bullish, find a stock that seems to follow the general trend. Buy a few shares, hold on to the position for a few points, and then close out the position. See if you can make a quick profit.

This strategy may seem simple and a little naïve, but sometimes such strategies have merit. Again, think of the surfer. When one is trying to ride a wave, he or she isn't concerned with why the wave occurs. He or she doesn't worry about when the next wave will come. Surfers simply try to find a wave, or an opportunity, get on it, and ride. They don't mull over issues, such as laws of motion according to classic physics or how gravity and the rotation of the planet influence the occurrence, height, or force of a wave. Such thinking is distracting. One doesn't need to understand why the wave comes in order to ride it. Some successful traders take a similar approach. At any given moment, one doesn't need to know why the stock price seems to be building momentum, but merely that it is building momentum. Traders get in, buy a few shares, and see if they can ride the trend to make a profit.

But just as the surfer isn't interested in being slammed into the sand, seasoned traders take precautions. They don't enter a trade without a well-defined plan. They have an idea of when they will buy, what technical indicators show that the price is in motion, and how they will exit once the trade is executed. They set a stop loss order or develop an exit point. They decide beforehand that they will get out of the trade if it goes against them. They don't wait until the last minute before taking action. And they don't risk it all on one trade. They manage their risk by limiting the amount of capital on any one trade to a small amount of their total trading capital. Similarly, a surfer wouldn't want to surf only one wave, destroy his or her board, or hurt oneself and not be able to surf again. The fun comes from surfing wave after wave. Similarly, a successful trader enjoys executing trade after trade and "riding" each "wave" or trading opportunity that presents itself.

It's useful to consider the surfing analogy when trading. Sometimes, there's a natural human tendency to make things more complicated than they need to be, and it's useful to simplify things.

All The Pieces Fit

Imagine that you're putting together a large jigsaw puzzle. You've worked on it everyday for weeks and you're almost done. You're down to your very last piece. You place it and stand back to look at the beautiful scenic picture, but you're dismayed. You've forgotten one piece. You allowed yourself to experience the pride of accomplishment too soon. Your initial exuberance now turns into anxiety and frustration.

You frantically look for the piece you may have missed, but you can't find it. You've looked everywhere to no avail. Hours pass and you start to accept the possibility that the missing piece will never be found. There's not much left to do: You must accept the fact that the one piece will remain missing. You console yourself. You look on the bright side, and appreciate what you have accomplished by almost completing the puzzle. But it's still not quite right; if you could have found the missing piece, you would feel much better - a lot more satisfied and accomplished.

A winning trade is very much like a completed jigsaw puzzle. Before you make the trade, you have signals, indicators, and ideas about the markets, just like you had the pieces before you started putting together the puzzle. You also had an idea of what a winning trade will be like. If all the pieces fit, you have a winning trade, but if you're missing one, you won't. You might be impressed or feel the pride of accomplishment about making whatever trade you made or perhaps about effectively cutting your losses before you lost too much, but the bottom line is, you didn't get that winning trade; you didn't get a chance to see the complete picture.

Although putting together a jigsaw puzzle is similar to putting together a winning trade, there are differences. When it comes to trading, you don't have any control over what pieces you get in the box. However, you do have complete control over the tools, indicators, signals, etc. that you choose to use and how you choose to use them. Many times, you identify what might be a good opportunity and evaluate it to find that most of the pieces are there, but a few are missing. If you pay close attention to your thought patterns throughout the trade, you'll find yourself being on the indecisive side and possibly even questioning your entry.

If you're a seasoned trader, you've most likely experienced what it feels like when all the pieces are there and fit: the trade goes smoothly and you have complete control. Your decisions are objective and accurate, and your timing is impeccable.

A Long and Winding Road

Trading requires getting in the zone; it's a flow experience. When seasoned traders place their trades, all their attention is focused on the trade. Their experiences are heightened and everything seems to click. Unless you are a seasoned trader who has experienced trading as a flow experience, getting a clear grasp of a flow experience is difficult. Fortunately, you've probably experienced many flow experiences in your everyday life, and you can use these prior experiences as a basis for understanding what a flow experience is. Driving a car is an activity that commonly produces a flow experience. Well, sometimes it is a flow experience and sometimes it is not. A flow experience is an optimal experience in that it is a challenge that does not exceed one's skills or resources. For an experienced driver, the task of driving is far from a flow experience. For example, driving in bumper-to-bumper rush hour traffic for 30 minutes doesn't take much skill at all. It's quite boring. Indeed, it's possible to do other tasks in addition to driving; many drivers can easily listen to a book on tape and increase their knowledge of a subject matter or learn a new language as they drive. Driving can be just plain boring at times, but some driving experiences are very similar to trading in the zone.

Consider driving at high speed down a long and winding road, like the Pacific Coast Highway. It's exciting to drive on this road. One minute you are driving a few miles away from the coast along a relatively straight passage through fields and farmland, while the next, you are driving along a winding 200-foot precipice on the edge of the ocean. If you make a mistake, you literally can plunge to your death. If you drive this road at the suggested speed limit, one can move in and out of a flow experience. Driving along the relatively straight passage can be like driving in rush hour traffic; it doesn't take much skill and it isn't a challenge. It can be quite boring and your mind can wander. On the other hand, driving too fast along the winding coastal passages is very dangerous.

It's clearly a flow experience. All your attention must be focused on making each turn at a speed that keeps your car on the road. If you drive too fast, you may miss the turn and fall to your death. You've got to anticipate each curve: Is there a truck in front of me? Can I cross over into the other lane if I need to? Is there oncoming traffic? Just how good is the car I'm driving? Just as with trading the markets, one needs to anticipate what can go wrong and be ready to take decisive action. As you drive through dangerous curves, it would not be wise to lose confidence. You've got to decide quickly what to do without much contemplation. When you are trying to make a turn at a high speed, you have to quickly make one of two choices: (a) decide that the turn exceeds your driving skills, hit the brakes, and take the curve at a slower speed or (b) decide the curve is within your skills, accelerate into the curve, and make it. As you are making the decision, it would be a big mistake to second-guess yourself, hesitate, and not take a decisive action. Your attention needs to be focused on what you are doing. Second-guessing breaks your train of thought. It interferes with your concentration. You've got to stay focused. The same holds for trading. There may be a tendency to become easily bored. At those times, you may fail to see the dangerous curves up ahead, or in trading, the potential adverse conditions that may turn the trade against you. You may also want to "slow down" at times and take the trading setups that don't exceed your skills. Make trading a flow experience. Find the happy medium between boredom and extreme challenge. If you can create a flow experience, you will see your profits grow.

The Sporting Life

Professionals at the top of their fields maximize their psychological resources. Professional athletes have known this for decades, and top traders are learning that consistent performers are in top physical and mental shape. Performance is dramatically enhanced if one has the right mental edge. We've all observed how this works on the playing field. Football teams with the proper mindset can turn a 21-point loss in the first half into a win, even if it means scoring a winning two-point conversion in the last

20 seconds of the game. Other teams can't recover if they don't build momentum in the first half. They drop the ball, throw an interception, and lose ground as the clock ticks away. Having the proper mindset can help you win the game of trading.

You've got to have the right mindset to trade profitably, day after day, and come out with a winning record, even when market conditions change. Many of the traders we have interviewed for our Master Interview series are former college or professional athletes who see a connection between trading and sports. Scott, for example, a Chicago-based trader and former University of Colorado Buffaloes' football player says, "a lot of this relates to athletics. You have to analyze what you're doing wrong. Sometimes it can be the market and sometimes it can just be a little bit of bad luck, but at the end of the day, you have to take each day separately, and try to steer clear of sticking them all together and saying, 'Boy, I've really stunk in the last 10 days.'" Andy, a former Cleveland Browns' linebacker equates trading to preparing for a football game: "The whole week you watch game films of the other team. You look for tendencies. You practice. When it comes to game time, you don't have to think. You have to react. Trading works the same way." Christopher, a trader based in Australia, sees trading as analogous to surfing: "You don't know when the next wave will come, but you know one will come eventually. When the right wave comes along, you need to be ready to ride it, take advantage of it, and make a win." What all of these traders know is that stock analysis alone will not make one a winning trader. One must be ready physically and mentally to be a winner.

Andy has noticed among participants in his seminars that former athletes tend to make good traders. It's probably because they are used to sticking to a game plan, recovering from setbacks easily, and are comfortable acting on their perceptions. They don't second-guess their decisions and actions. Instead, they develop some key support and resistance levels, come up with a plan, and go into the markets to see what patterns and setups are consistent with that plan. When they see a setup that will work with their plan, they act decisively, without hesitation or doubt. Since they have protection of their capital through proper risk management, they are not worried if they make a mistake. They can recover quickly and take advantage of the next opportunity, or "ride the next good wave" to use Christopher's surfing analogy. It's useful to think about how trading is similar to playing a sport. Considering these similarities and applying them to your trading style may help you improve your trading performance.

Chapter 2

Positive Mindset

It's hard to be successful. It's hard to be above average. Trading is difficult, and if it were easy, everyone would be making millions. Having a positive mindset is vital for success. People who don't have an optimistic or positive mindset are not successful. They don't persist. They give up easily. There is often a vast difference, however, between thinking positively and thinking realistically. Thinking positively concerns trusting your abilities, having confidence in your methods, and putting your honed skills to work. But this is only realistic if you have the skills to back it up. If you don't have the trading skills, then you may be thinking positively, but you are also deluding yourself.

There are at least two types of people when it comes to a positive outlook. The first type has faced many challenges and has learned to overcome them and gained success. These people are happy most of the time and generally satisfied with life. They make optimal traders because they are not out to prove their abilities to others. They know they are successful. They are sure of themselves and have deep beliefs in their abilities. They don't question their self-worth and don't believe, or don't care, that others are testing their worth.

The other type of person has low self-esteem. Somewhere and somehow, these individuals learned that they had little worth. They were told that they have no value. And now, they question their self-worth. They believe things won't go their way. They are cautious and skeptical, and they are never quite sure of their abilities. They question themselves. They doubt themselves. They vacillate between extreme overconfidence and extreme self-doubt and despair. They are prone to question themselves and doubt their abilities. They tend to think pessimistically most times, and they struggle to cultivate a positive mindset.

This chapter is a collection of essays about developing a positive mindset. One must be an optimist to trade successfully. But that's only one half of the equation. One can't be too optimistic in this game. The next chapter on overconfidence is a good companion. The ongoing challenge is to find the proper balance between humility and overconfidence.

Developing Positive Self-Worth

Personal Integrity: A Pillar of Self-Esteem

Successful traders have high self-esteem. They've got to. Trading skills are hard to develop and much easier when one has high self-esteem. People with low self-esteem have not developed high regard for themselves. Throughout their lives, they have tended to compromise their ideals and seek out guidance and direction from others. By doing so, they have often been exploited, and by the time they become traders, they are out to prove their self-worth. They want to show others that they shouldn't have been mistreated, and that they can gain mastery over their domain.

It's dangerous to be in this position. Since trading is not an arena where most people are winners, many traders with low self-esteem are setting themselves up for failure. It's vital to determine whether one of your motives for trading is to raise your self-esteem.

Here is a brief assessment that addresses personal integrity, which is a pillar of self-esteem. See how well you do.

In this exercise, you will be presented with two moral dilemmas. Read each carefully and respond as honestly as possible. Write down your responses. The purpose of this exercise is to increase your awareness, so think about how you would actually behave in the situation, rather than how you would prefer to behave.

Moral dilemma A: You are a member of a club that is very important to you. Many of your close friends are members. You greatly admire the president of the club. John, a very close friend of yours, has recently had a falling out with the president. He resigns his membership and the president tells everyone to avoid any further contact with John. What would you do? Would you avoid any further contact with John or would you listen to his side of the story and decide what to do next? Would you still be friends with John even though the rest of the group ostracized him?

Moral dilemma B: Your company is bidding on a contract that could fund your department for the next two years. Without this contract, you will lose your job. The funding decision hinges on a final presentation by the head of your department to a government agency. There are several flaws with your company's manufacturing plans, and the head of your department avoids talking about these issues. When one of these flaws is raised, your department head deceives the director of the government agency. On the one hand, the jobs of you and your fellow employees are at stake, but on the other hand, other people's lives and taxpayer dollars are at stake should this deception continue. What would you do? Clarify the deception? Say nothing and justify the action? Say nothing at the presentation, but resign in protest?

Personal integrity is a critical component of self-esteem. Integrity concerns the consistency between our values and actions. It's often easier to bow to social pressure and avoid conflict, but we pay a price for such behavior: we lower our self-esteem. What did you do in these moral dilemmas? Did you yield to authority and social pressure or did you look toward your own values for how to behave? If you succumbed to social pressure or authority, you may have low self-esteem. People with high self-esteem, and especially seasoned traders, follow their own instincts rather than looking toward others. Consider where you stand.

The Success Identity

Everyone must find his or her identity. They must determine who they are, their place in the world, and just where they fit in. People with low self-esteem are often those individuals who don't have a clearly defined identity. Throughout their lives, they were told that they don't matter and will not succeed. They learned early in life to put a low value on their worth. They believe that success is not deserved, and must continually prove their value to themselves and others. Dr. William Glasser (1965) has said such individuals have a "failure identity" rather than a "success identity." Why do people hold on to a failure identity, rather than build a new success identity? It's sometimes easier to have a failure identity than no identity at all. One becomes accustomed to being a failure and to thinking in such terms. It's a vicious cycle of sorts. The person was treated as if he or she was a failure while developing a sense of self, so he or she fulfilled this prophecy by acting like a failure. The individual with the failure identity then approaches new tasks under the assumption that he or she will fail, and so he or she ends up failing, which in turn reinforces the failure identity.

People with a success identity, in contrast, know how to succeed when pursuing a new endeavor. They don't view success as merely a given. They know that success entails careful planning, hard work, and commitment. Success doesn't happen overnight. They know this because they have been successful in other endeavors. The advantage they have over the people with a failure identity is not just a positive attitude, although they have one; it's having the confidence to know that if they put in a heroic effort, they will come out ahead. They know that they have to make careful plans, develop skills, and practice them. For example, when it comes to trading, they aren't overconfident. They aren't fooled by the brokerage commercials or trading books that portray trading as "easy money," but at the same time, they don't make it overly complicated. They know that by setting realistic goals, taking risks, and practicing their methods, they will come out a winner. It may not be tomorrow, it may not be next month, but someday, they know they will be a success. They take a step-by-step methodical approach. They don't set vague lofty goals, such as, "I'm going to make a million dollars trading, buy a big house and a luxury car, and show everyone that I'm a big shot." That's thinking too far into the future. Successful people just take it one day at a time. They plan carefully and enjoy the experience of achieving their goals, step by step.

People with a "failure identity" do the exact opposite. They are unsure of themselves and vacillate between extreme confidence and no confidence at all. They hope and dream of success and believe that all it takes is a "positive attitude" to be successful. But people with a success identity know it isn't that easy. They expect to fail. They know from experience that "one must fall before one learns to run." That's true in other areas of life and it's true of trading.

So don't approach trading with a failure identity. Create realistic goals. Gauge your performance accurately. Study trading methods and practice a few. But most importantly, be ready to hone your skills. Don't expect overnight success. Practice, study, and try again. You may fail at times, but just pick yourself up and try again. Over time, you will build a "success identity" when it comes to trading.

Fluctuations in Self-Esteem

Self-esteem is related to success as a trader. It's hard to be an effective trader if one has low self-esteem. In a general sense, self-esteem can be viewed as a personality trait. As a result of past experiences, people with high self-esteem learned to view themselves as having self worth, and thus, self-esteem. Once they decide they have value, and self-worth, they continue to hold themselves in high regard no matter what events occur afterward. They no longer believe they have to prove their worth to themselves or anyone else. They don't make their self-worth contingent on other people or events. People with low self-esteem, in contrast, may believe that they don't deserve respect. People with low self-esteem may seek out respect from others and act as if they need to prove to themselves and to others that they are worthy. Traders with low self-esteem may try to prove their worth with each trade. It's as if they are thinking, "If I can be a winner as a trader, I'll show everyone that I'm worthy of their respect." The difficulty with this thinking is that they are placing their self-worth on the line with each trade. That puts a lot of pressure on oneself and often leads to disaster.

Some researchers have questioned the notion of self-esteem as a personality trait, which is stable across time and across situations. Even persons with high self-esteem may feel they have low self-esteem occasionally, especially when they experience a string of failures. For example, a trader with high self-esteem may start to doubt his or her abilities after facing a bout of losing trades from which he or she could not recover. A recent study by Dr. Jennifer Crocker and colleagues demonstrates that self-esteem may vary as a function of success and failure (Crocker, Sommers, & Luhtanen, 2002). They studied 38 college seniors with high self-esteem and outstanding scholastic performance who applied to several competitive graduate school programs. Self-esteem was measured twice a week for two months. Although participants had high self-esteem, there was a tendency to base some of their self-worth on whether or not they gained acceptance to graduate programs. This is reasonable, considering that to these participants, admission to graduate school was an important life goal. Nevertheless, some students put a lot of their self-esteem on the line with each application they submitted, while others did not. As you might expect, self-esteem was associated with acceptance to graduate school. That is, self-esteem was higher after a success than a failure. What's interesting, however, is that this effect depended on the extent persons allowed their self-worth to be dictated by whether or not they were accepted into graduate school. People who believed that their self-worth did not depend on whether they succeeded or failed were less influenced by whether they were actually accepted into graduate school. It's as if they did not put their self-esteem on the line with each application to graduate school. By not doing so, they did not allow the outcome to influence their feelings of self-worth.

These findings have a direct bearing on trading. If you place your self-esteem on the line with each trading outcome, your feelings of self-esteem will fluctuate with your successes and failures. The key to successful trading is to remove self-esteem from the picture. Don't place your self-worth on the line with each winning or losing trade. Remember that you have self-worth and value, no matter how many losing trades you encounter. Follow the old adage, "Don't define your self-worth by your net worth."

Cultivating a Positive Mindset

Maintaining a Carefree Attitude

The proper mindset can go far to improve one's trading results. Successful traders have a carefree attitude when it comes to trading. They have little difficulty executing trades. They don't second-guess their decisions and they are not overly influenced by their emotions. How does one develop a carefree attitude? Let's review some of the necessary conditions.

Look at the bigger picture: Don't focus on the outcome of a single trade. Think of the bigger picture. You may lose on a single trade, but across a series of trades, you will come out ahead, if you have a trading strategy that works part of the time. Successful traders plan on executing many trades and know that not all trades need to be winners in order to increase the equity in their accounts. It's your success overall that matters. Keeping this in mind takes some of the pressure off.

Use proper risk management: Successful traders risk only a small percentage of their trading capital on a single trade. Limiting the risk on a single trade further relieves some of the pressure to feel that every trade needs to be a winner.

Don't be afraid to admit you are wrong: Maladaptive beliefs can be a trader's worst enemy. Many times, one may think, "I can't be wrong on this trade" or "I must capitalize on every opportunity to make a profit." These expectations are so high that they can cause fear and anxiety. When you hold such high expectations for your performance, you place too much pressure on yourself, and cannot maintain a carefree attitude.

Gain awareness of personal conflicts and try to resolve them: The desire to resolve unmet psychological needs interferes with maintaining a carefree attitude. Examples of psychological needs include the need for self-worth, the need to prove one's value, or the need for close personal relationships. These needs must be satisfied in a satisfactory manner in order to maintain a carefree attitude. If these needs are not met, one is likely to secretly wish that by winning big in the markets, conflicts arising from these unmet needs will be miraculously resolved. It doesn't work that way. Performance in the markets cannot help one satisfy these needs, and believing that they will, consciously or unconsciously, can be the greatest interference for maintaining a carefree attitude.

Following these guidelines will help put you on your way to developing the carefree attitude associated with trading success.

Be In the Moment

One of the central requirements for successful trading is an intense connection to current market realities. The most successful traders are the ones who feel every nuance of market psychology and behavior, and who don't let their hopes or dreams mask the actual trends and patterns the market is tracing out, moment by moment. To remain in the moment as you are trading, try these ideas:

Stay in touch with your gut feelings: Top traders have a *golden gut* that tells them what is relevant, what is important, and what is not. Because they are intensely aware of their own feelings, sensibilities, and judgments, they can review thousands of details and unerringly select the very few that are most likely to drive market action. Your gut can take on more of a golden hue, too, if you will take the time to keep asking yourself what you really feel, and keep listening as carefully as you can for your answers.

Delay thoughts about past and future successes: It is inevitable that you will want to think about what you can buy with your earnings, or how much you might pocket if a certain trade works out. But thoughts like these take you out of the moment, and weaken your connection to the current mood of the market. Save them for weekends and vacations. When you are trading, analyzing past trades, and preparing for future trades, keep your thoughts focused as tightly as you can on the most immediate considerations.

Don't be self-conscious: If you are like most traders, you can find your way into a flow state in which your most effective trading just happens; without conscious thought, you see an opportunity, and you just take it. But you take yourself out of this flow when you allow self-conscious thoughts, such as, "I wish I could tell someone how great I'm doing" to intrude. The less self-conscious you can remain in this flow state, the more effectively you will be able to trade.

Keeping It Simple

Henry David Thoreau was fond of saying, “Simplify, Simplify.” He preached returning to basics, living in nature, and living the simple life. He wasn’t talking about trading strategies, but one could say the same about trading, in a metaphorical sense. In recent years, traders have acquired complicated computer software, multiple technical indicators, and many different sources of data. Some traders who remember the “old days” of having to read actual paper charts advise, “Simplify, Simplify.” It’s useful to remember to return to the basics and look at the markets in more simple and basic terms.

Many technical indicators are quite similar and redundant. They indicate parameters, such as sentiment and trend. It’s tempting to look at multiple indicators, however. For many people, “complete and perfect” information, along with the mastery of complex information, means safety and security. Although some traders endlessly search for the Holy Grail of easy money, other traders believe that trading is more complex than it actually is. They believe it’s as complex as physics or biology. It’s as if they are thinking, “If I could just understand all of the technical indicators and use them to analyze my charts, I could identify the right pattern, and I could predict with certainty what the market will do next.” Unfortunately, the markets don’t work that way. There is less certainty in the markets than in physical sciences. One can’t predict with absolute certainty no matter what analyses one conducts.

In modern society, technology, and the complexity associated with it, has improved our lives, and we sometimes believe this has a direct bearing on our trading strategies. We believe that because advanced technology for conducting our analyses is available, its use will improve our analyses. It may now be easier to “crunch” data and “read” charts with the use of advanced charting software, but it’s also important to remember that more complex and comprehensive analysis does not mean more predictability. By looking at multiple, yet redundant, indicators of the same parameters, you may feel more confident, but it doesn’t mean you can predict the markets with any more accuracy. That’s not to say that one should not look at a few key indicators, but keep in mind that more may not mean better. Don’t fall prey to the fallacy of thinking complex is better and more analysis means more predictability. An unfortunate reality of trading is that the markets are hard to predict. Many unknown variables may influence prices, and there are many traders out there who as a collective can influence prices as well. At best, prediction is an educated guess based on the available information that you realistically can process at any given time. Information isn’t absolute and it's not perfect. With that in mind, it makes sense to "simplify" your trading strategy. Look at a few key indicators, manage your risk, and see how many trading opportunities you can capitalize on. Don't get bogged down with complexity: Simplify, Simplify.

Just Do Your Best

When overwhelmed by an ambitious goal, one often hears the advice, "Don't put so much pressure on yourself, just do the best you can do." This advice is reassuring. It makes you feel good. Stress, distress, and despair are now replaced with relief and contentment. It's like being given permission, or giving yourself permission, to give up the more difficult goal and try to achieve a goal that is more attainable. In a recent review of the scientific literature, Drs. Edwin Locke and Gary Latham (2002) point out that merely "doing your best" can have dire consequences for performance: when people are asked to "do your best," they often do not do so. Instead, they set goals that are too easy, and much lower than people who set higher goals and push themselves in order to reach them.

On the surface, "doing the best you can do" seems similar to saying, "I let the markets tell me how much profit I can make." One certainly shouldn't pretend there are good trading opportunities when there are not, but on the other hand, just trying to do your best and nothing more may lead to an underestimation of opportunities, settling for a repertoire of relatively ineffective trading strategies, or accepting a low level of performance. It may be better to set one's standards a little higher.

In setting goals, it's important to separate a *learning* goal from a *performance* goal. If you are a skilled and seasoned trader, you can set a high *performance goal* (such as achieving a high return per month). Seasoned traders have a repertoire of trading methods that can be used "automatically" without taxing limited psychological resources. The methods are so heavily practiced that they can be implemented with success by merely using them. It doesn't make sense to "just try to do your best" with this level of skill. One can set a relatively high goal for one's performance and try to achieve it. For such individuals, trying to achieve high levels of performance energize, direct, and allow one to persist even under the most severe circumstances.

If you are a novice trader who does not have a high level of trading skills, it isn't a very good idea to set a high performance goal. You can't attain it. Trying to attain a goal that exceeds your skills will make you feel stressed out and worried. But this doesn't mean you should not set high goals for yourself. Instead of setting a performance goal, set a *learning* goal. Plan on learning new trading strategies and practicing them so as to hone your skills. For example, you may decide to spend four hours a day reading about new technical indicators, or trying out two new strategies a month (using small amounts of capital and risk management). Goals direct and energize your behavior. By having a very specific learning goal (not a performance goal), you will push yourself to develop your trading methods, over-practice them, and use them to achieve a high performance goal later.

Goal setting can do a lot to increase your trading performance, but the key is to know what kinds of goals to set and when. Seasoned traders can set high performance goals, since they have the experience and the skills. Novice traders don't have the skills yet, but by having high learning goals, they can develop the skills, and someday use these skills to achieve high performance goals.

Thinking in Terms of Probabilities

Successful traders think in terms of probabilities. Rather than looking at the outcome of a single trade by itself, they view it as merely one outcome among a set of outcomes. They believe that overall their trading strategy will give them an edge, and allow them to come out ahead if they make enough trades.

Probability theory is concerned with hypothetical outcomes of a process that can be repeated over and over again, forever. For example, suppose one were to toss a coin an infinite number of times. There are two possible outcomes: heads or tails. Thus, if a fair coin were tossed an infinite number of times, one would expect heads to occur 50% of the time and tails to occur 50% of the time. Since the outcome of one toss is independent of the outcome of any other toss, it is impossible to predict the outcome of any single toss. However, with a large enough number of tosses, one would expect about half will be heads and half will be tails.

Suppose that you received $2 each time the coin landed on heads and lost $1 each time the coin landed on tails. Assuming that you toss the coin a sufficient number of times, you will come out ahead. As an interesting exercise, toss a coin 10 times. You will find that sometimes, you will come out ahead, sometimes you will be behind, and sometimes you will break even. This happens because 10 tosses are not very many tosses compared to an infinite number of tosses. The 50/50 chance of obtaining heads is only based on an infinite number of tosses, but you will see the more tosses you make, the closer the resulting distribution of outcomes will approach a 50/50 split.

Trading outcomes can be looked at in the same way. If one were to view trading outcomes as tossing a coin, one could not predict the outcome of a single trade, but across a long series of trades, one could expect a 50/50 split, assuming a trading strategy works 50% of the time it is used.

In terms of cultivating a positive mindset, thinking in terms of probabilities is useful. It's useful to think, "the more trades I make, the closer the outcomes will be to the expected performance of the trading strategy." But on the other hand, such an assumption may predispose one to be overconfident. Who really knows what the "true" performance, or odds of success will be. The true performance is based on using an infinite number of times, and the number of times one uses a trading strategy under practical market conditions is far less than infinity. In a purely mathematical sense, it isn't possible to estimate the odds that a trading strategy is expected to produce a win, since the strategy cannot be repeated an infinite number of times. The best we can do is use historical data to see how well the trading strategy has worked in the past, and assume it will work in the future when similar market conditions exist. Ideally, historical data should provide evidence that your strategy will give you enough of an "edge" to come out ahead. But the past doesn't necessarily predict the future. And in the markets, it rarely does, so under what basis should you believe that scientifically you have an edge? There is no basis, mathematically or scientifically. But it's useful for cultivating a positive mindset.

From a psychological sense, it is useful to view the outcomes of trading strategies as independent outcomes in the same way that a coin is tossed over and over again. It isn't useful to isolate the outcome of a single trade, worry that the trading strategy failed, and produced a loss. Even if trading were like flipping a coin, you wouldn't think the coin is biased just because it produced heads on five flips of a coin. You would toss it many more times before you started to believe it was biased. The same can be said of a trading strategy. Don't abandon it prematurely. Stick with it a little longer and give it a fair chance to produce a profit.

Focusing on an outcome as just one outcome in a series of outcomes also eases some of the pressure. You will not tend to think that every trade needs to be a winner, which can be very stressful, and you will be more relaxed if you look at the bigger picture. Thinking in terms of probabilities can help you cultivate a positive mindset.

A Winning Attitude

Successful traders have a winning attitude. It's not simply that they expect to win, although they do expect it. It's not simply that they have the confidence that comes with a winning track record, although they have one. It is more important that they have the calm, patient skill and expertise of someone who is doing everything it takes to win. Meanwhile, traders who are struggling without much luck to do better than the crowd are failing to capture the big gains and are falling prey to the traps that net them large losses. Developing and maintaining a "winning attitude" takes time and effort. But it pays off big in terms of getting you positioned for major gains and keeping you away from major losses. To improve your daily trading results, try nurturing the following elements of the winning attitude:

Improve your skills and expertise: Success in trading does not come haphazardly. It finds and stays with those who have studied the markets, mastered their methods, and prepared in depth for the trading day. As you develop your level of skills and expertise, you will automatically begin to develop the same winning attitude as the top traders of the world. The more you experience success, the more you will learn to trust yourself. You will know from first hand experience that your skills produce positive results, and once you truly see what you can do, your self-confidence will solidify rather than wax and wane with each winning and losing day.

Cultivate your calmness: High emotion, panic, frenzy, and anxiety tend to make success in the markets more difficult to achieve. That is why the most successful traders tend to be unflappable, no matter what is going on around them. You will gain an extra measure of calm automatically as your confidence level increases. But take preventative measures to inoculate yourself from stressful events. Practice stress relaxation techniques, such as taking a deep breath before responding to a situation; meditate regularly and practice relaxing your muscles and your mind.

It's How You React

One of the central realizations for traders on their march toward increased levels of success is that the markets are simply too big to control. There is no way to move prices, change trends, revise the perceptions of others, or otherwise make the markets perform closer to the way you would like. In fact, the only part of the markets, or life in general, you can ever control is how you act, and how you react to events. Let's concentrate for the moment on your reactions. Say you have some positions open, and the market goes wildly against you. In one quick move, it shatters all your assumptions, and proves all your expectations false. Clearly, you are in the middle of an upsetting day. Most people would have a hard time dealing with the stress, and maintaining their composure and control. If you want to be a successful trader, however, you'll use some or all of the following techniques to control your reactions:

Lessen your anxiety: Unwanted and unpleasant events generally trigger strong anxiety reactions, which in turn make it more difficult to formulate effective responses. Your first move should be to shut down as much of the anxiety you are feeling as possible. You may do this by conscious relaxation techniques, taking a break, or going to your support network for advice. But it is important to cut back on the anxiety you are feeling before you begin making important decisions.

Correct your interpretation: Adverse market events often appear to be one thing when they are actually something else. Rather than reacting to first impressions, successful traders usually take time to determine the facts, to think clearly about what they know, and to reach some conclusions about what it all means. Remember, your results do not depend solely on how quickly you make decisions, but also on how accurately you make them.

Lessen the impact of past traumatic events: Untutored traders allow many past memories and associations to influence their current reactions to major events. You may not be reacting just to the market downturn, but also to memories of how your parents treated you badly, for example. The result is that your reactions are not as razor sharp, as pinpointed, or as astutely accurate as they should be. It is important to gain awareness of these memories and associations in advance of major turning points in your trading career, so you can have them at least somewhat under control before they can drive you away from your desired goals.

Find new ways of responding: The biggest mistake is to think you haven't grown and your only recourse to unwanted and unpleasant events is to respond as you did years ago. But successful traders know they have many choices of how to react, and they carefully select the one that is most likely to bring them the results they want.

Do It Yourself Trading

One of the keys to successful trading is to get in tune with your own investment psychology. That is, you can never be as successful trading according to other people's ideas and trigger points as you can trading according to your own.

Certainly, it's easier and simpler when you're starting out to follow the lead of a proven, successful trader. It's also more comfortable to go with the herd or to bet on the basis of a rumor or supposedly "inside information."

But in the long run, trading in this "second hand" way will limit your satisfaction, cut into your psychological strength and commitment to trading, and ultimately put a cap on your success.

Among the reasons that trading according to your own insights, ideas, and judgment works better, you'll find:

You'll own the trades: Following the best advice from the world's sharpest trader is inferior to trading according to your own insights, ideas, and judgment for the same sort of reasons that working for yourself is better than working for someone else. When you call your own trades, you feel better about them. You'll also be fully aware of the reasons for taking each trade, and of how a change in any market condition or variable impacts the trade and the value of staying in it. This will give you far more flexibility to adjust to changing market conditions than you can possibly have by following the directions of someone else.

You'll strengthen your mental edge: Self-sufficiency is an important trait that makes for better results not only in trading, but also in all aspects of work and life. As you become adept at trading according to your own insights, ideas, and judgment, you'll be building and sharpening powerful mental edges that will help you succeed in far more situations than just the market.

You'll take full responsibility: It's the difference between taking orders and giving orders. In one case, you have to be grateful to someone else for your winnings in the market; and be wary that they could dry up at any time. In the other case, you can feel good about your own ability to generate profits, and feel very comfortable and confident that you can do it whenever you wish.

You'll move away from the herd: Perhaps most important, there are bigger profits to be made on the outskirts of market action than in the mainstream.

While following others' ideas and trading with the herd can bring you profits, developing and pursuing your own ideas for when and what to trade is more likely to produce a huge pile of winnings.

Timely Action

To every thing there is a season. Nowhere is this more relevant than for trading, where the smallest hesitation that prevents you from acting at just the right time can sap the strength out of a winning opportunity and spell the difference between success and failure. Unfortunately, there is no easy way to discern when the time is right for action and when it is better to hold back from pulling the trigger in favor of more investigation, analysis, and contemplation of your options. But there are some guidelines you can bear in mind as you try to wring all the unwanted hesitation out of your trading:

Don't overthink it: It is important to think through a trading opportunity and draw an actionable conclusion on a timely basis. But when you find yourself thinking and rethinking the same facts, reevaluating the same options, and redrawing the same conclusions more than once or twice, you are probably overthinking the situation and hesitating when you should be trading.

Don't spend more time than it is worth: Many unsuccessful traders spend hours and hours of their valuable time thinking about whether or not to open a test-size trade that risks, at most, a few hundred dollars. That is not a good use of your time. On smaller trades, it is almost better simply to open a position and watch what it does. Gather additional evidence and give yourself a gut-level feel for the market.

Don't dwell on mistakes: Emotionally, you can cause problems for yourself in the future if you allow yourself to dwell on mistakes you have made in the past. By all means, learn what you can from your errors. Certainly, you should never forget what your experience has taught you. But if your errors morph into living nightmares, they will cripple your ability to make trading decisions effectively and quickly as future opportunities present themselves.

A Totally Open Mind

One of the major differences between successful and unsuccessful traders is having a "totally open mind." Think about it: the average person believes the sky will not fall, his or her account balances will stay high, and that today will proceed pretty much as yesterday and the day before. The successful trader, in contrast, assumes nothing is a sure thing. He or she is ready for earth-shattering changes every day. More than ready, he or she is watching for them, and hoping to spot them before anyone else so as to turn a profit from the observation and quick action. Some of the psychological elements that allow you to cultivate and maintain a "totally open mind" include:

A fact-based outlook on life: Traders are inherently rooted in reality. To cultivate a totally open mind, try to pay attention to what is really going on in situations, particularly situations where you may be fooling yourself to avoid an uncomfortable fact or two. What are people really saying? What forces are really at work? What are the probabilities of each possible occurrence?

Enough confidence that change doesn't scare you: The courage to accept an uncertain and rapidly changing future comes only from confidence that you will be able to handle the changes successfully. Build this kind of confidence by tracking your successes, not only in trading, but in life. The greater the proportion of your self-reflective thoughts that dwell on triumphs, rather than failures, the more your confidence will increase. Overconfidence can be a problem, but we will discuss that in the next chapter.

Willingness to change course: Many people like to anticipate their actions far in advance, and once they have a plan of action in mind, they prefer not to make changes. Sometimes, they simply refuse. But traders with a totally open mind are perfectly willing to rethink their action plans, revise their anticipated activities, and redo their open positions as often as conditions may warrant. They accept that even the most definite plan is only "tentative" until the moment comes for actually executing it.

A Firm Direction

One of the central elements of a successful trader's process is a clear understanding of what he or she wants to accomplish and how. In other professions, this might be called a "business plan," "strategic plan," or "mission statement." But in trading, you can get away without the formal written document, as long as you do the thinking that lies behind it. The main topics to think about include:

Your ultimate goal(s): Forget the money. That's a given. What else must you achieve to consider yourself a "success"? To paraphrase W. Edwards Deming, a guru of modern industry, "It's not enough to be in business just to make money. You must want to accomplish something you believe in, and then find a way to make money doing that." As a trader, success will certainly take the form of money. But aside from that, are you motivated to acquire certain expertise, understand certain market mechanisms, or develop a particular indicator or method that helps your trading? Find something important you care about and can strive for.

Your route to the goal(s): Once you know your goal(s), it's far easier every day to see whether you're heading in the right direction or not. With your goal(s) in mind, you can also think ahead, and plan out a route that continually brings you closer. In trading, this route might involve drilling yourself in the price relationships among certain financial instruments, learning the parameters of profitable setups in certain markets, studying the trading habits of certain market makers in hopes of trading with or against them, or something entirely different. With a sensible route mapped out, you can begin to consciously spend time following that route, and stop yourself whenever you wander too far off the track.

Your interim milestones: Most of us do our best work when we get frequent feedback that we are doing the right thing. With a route to follow, one of your first tasks should be to establish important milestones that are clear, fixed, and objective. As you progress in your trading, keep checking to see when you reach each one. This way, at any given moment, you can easily see how much progress you have made along your route to success.

Your daily means to the goal(s): It's difficult, but it is an important benefit of having a firm direction: Simply giving yourself one or more clear-cut goals to accomplish every day often boosts your level of success. If one of your trading goals is to master the complex relationships between options and their underlying stocks, for example, you'll never do it in one step. So it's worthwhile to break up your larger goal into smaller steps, and complete one step each day. It will help you feel confident that you are making progress toward your ultimate goal(s).

Chapter 3

Overconfidence

Overconfidence is cited as one of the most prevalent problems traders face. But "overconfidence" is rarely defined, and perspectives differ depending upon the professional or academic discipline one uses to understand overconfidence. The definitions and explanations for overconfidence are quite varied. In this chapter, we explore overconfidence from several perspectives, from informal psychodynamic perspectives to formal behavioral finance perspectives. It's useful to consider the various perspectives one can take when attempting to understand overconfidence. Some approaches may apply to all traders to some extent, while others may apply to only a small subset of traders. As you read through this collection of essays, evaluate each one and decide which approach you prefer.

What is Overconfidence?

A Big Ego: The Psychodynamic View

Having a "big ego" can be a problem for trading. You've probably heard that time and time again. What does it mean to have a big ego? This is a colloquial term rather than a formal psychological one, but it usually refers to a person who has an overly high regard for his or her talents and abilities. People with big egos think they are more talented than they really are. They believe they are invincible, unique, and deserving of special treatment. Why is this? Why is it a detriment for trading? What's the cure for a big ego?

Let's start by considering the question, "What is a big ego?" Freud introduced the ego in his psychoanalytic theory of personality. The psyche consists of three parts: id, superego, and ego. The id is the animal side of personality: the desire for pleasure, sex, and aggression. The superego consists of values, ideals, and one's conscience. There is often a conflict between the desires of the id and the superego: that is, the practical social restrictions placed on the needs of the id, along with conflicts based on one's values. The ego acts as a mediator when a conflict arises between the id and the superego. From a Freudian point of view, one trades to make money, which in turn, allows one to gain pleasure and satisfy the basic human needs of the id (Many psychologists believe the Freudian view is a little too animalistic; human nature may be more about striving for a higher level of existence than satisfying basic needs, so take this discussion with a grain of salt). One of the ego's main goals is self-preservation, so any threat to the ego is warded off with an ego defense mechanism, such as denial (pretending a threat doesn't exist) or reaction formation (behaving in a way that is opposite to one's true feelings). For example, a looming trading loss is a threat to the ego, since a significant loss will not allow the satisfaction of basic pleasurable impulses. To ward off this threat, one may deny the threat exists, or use reaction formation, which is similar to saying, "I'm not afraid of the loss, see how self-assured and confident I am." Reaction formation is an example of having a big ego. One is secretly afraid of the loss and its implications, so one denies it and exaggerates one's talents to deal with it: The more extreme the threat, the stronger the reaction.

Anyone can be threatened so greatly that one's ego defense mechanisms are invoked, but some people are more easily threatened than others. Some are more prone to a big ego in that they are easily threatened and are prone to exaggerate their abilities as a form of self-protection. Having a big ego can be a problem for trading. Successful trading requires a firm grounding in reality. People with a big ego deny and distort reality; protection of the self is more important than accurate perception.

How does one defeat a big ego? It isn't easy. Ego defensive processes are usually unconscious and difficult to bring into awareness. But the best approach is to be aware of the process. Realize that a big ego occurs when one feels the most threatened. Any way of reducing threat to the ego will prevent ego defense mechanisms from being invoked. So when you have a big ego, realize that you are probably the most afraid. Rather than deny you are afraid, admit it. This will help you bring down your "big ego" to an appropriate level.

The Behavioral View

You've been watching a stock for three hours and you tell yourself, "It seems to match perfectly to the first two waves of an Elliott Wave pattern. I've seen this before and I've made big profits every time. It's so close that it's got to be a match. I'm getting in. I think I'm right. How can I be wrong? I'm positive that I've got this one pinned down." Sometimes, it's hard to know if you are right or wrong when it comes to a trading decision. Are you overconfident? Are you not confident enough? Overconfidence is one of the biggest psychological issues for traders, and depending on the school of thought, psychologists differ as to the explanations of overconfidence. From the psychodynamic viewpoint, over-confidence is a result of a "big ego." But from the behavioral perspective, it's a matter of learned behavior.

Your trading experience may tell you that overconfidence coincides with a set of thoughts, feelings and emotions, but that is irrelevant from the vantage point of a radical behaviorist. All that matters is how behaviors are rewarded, or "reinforced." Overconfident traders are usually those traders who had a lot of wins (or reinforcement) in their early trades. Because past trading behavior, regardless of skill level, was rewarded, it persists, even under circumstances of low reward.

Psychologist B. F. Skinner introduced the idea that our current behavior is the result of past "reinforcement contingencies." Skinner studied laboratory animals, such as rats and pigeons, to determine how rewards can "shape" behavior. For example, when a laboratory animal is given a food pellet every time it presses a lever, the rate of lever pressing is high. Translated into familiar terms of trading, when a trading strategy produces a profit, it is likely to be repeated. Albert Bandura (1977), author of social learning theory, refined Skinner's theory by noting that humans tend to "encode" and remember past reward contingencies. They develop expectations of reward and use these expectations to decide whether to repeat a behavior or not. Thus, it may not matter what the actual reward contingencies were that originally influenced a trading behavior, but the expectation of reward in the future.

Overconfidence is the expectation that trading behaviors will be positively rewarded. Skinner found that a "partial reinforcement" reward schedule produces behavior that is hard to change. When the laboratory animal is reinforced for every third lever press, for example, the animal persists, even when the behavior is no longer rewarded. A slot machine works on a similar principle. Jackpots are awarded sporadically, so people are not sure when they will be rewarded and when they will not. When it comes to trading, trading methods associated with sporadic profits are more likely to be used. The most overconfident people are those individuals who are inconsistently rewarded. Their trading strategies are rewarded sporadically, so they never know exactly when the strategy will produce a profit and when it will not. They continue to use these strategies, even though they are unlikely to produce rewards.

It's useful to be aware of the various explanations for overconfidence. Each explanation has a grain of truth to it, and it's useful to decide how your overconfidence may be explained by it. From the behavioral perspective, overconfidence is a matter of believing that one will receive rewards, just because one has received them in the past. But one may not receive rewards in the future; it's not simply a matter of believing you will be rewarded. One's expectations may be false. Trading strategies that have a successful track record are notorious for failing to work in the future. So your past learning history may be a poor predictor of the future. One of the best ways to beat overconfidence is to remember that merely believing you will be rewarded does not guarantee that you will be rewarded.

Cognitive Information Processing

Overconfidence is ubiquitous among traders. There are several explanations for overconfidence, depending on the psychological theory one uses to understand it. We've looked at overconfidence from the psychodynamic and behavioral perspectives. But behavioral economists have proposed one of the most popular theories: Overconfidence is a result of problems with humans' ability to process information.

Humans process information in a way that is similar to how computers analyze, retain, store, and retrieve information. But people sometimes have limitations when it comes to information processing capacity. They can't process all possible available information, so they rely on "heuristics" or "rules of thumb," which process information quickly and efficiently, but are often wrong. Overconfidence occurs when traders don't have enough time or resources to process information adequately. They act on inadequate information and make mistakes. Sometimes, they act on some form of popular opinion.

Let's consider a classic exercise that is used to demonstrate overconfidence in everyday decision-making. Answer the following questions: Are people more likely to die from asthma or tornadoes? Most people would say tornadoes and be very confident about their decision. It seems that we hear about fatalities from tornadoes all the time, but who ever dies from asthma? We use the available knowledge to make our judgment. Actually, 1996 statistics show that out of 1 billion people, 920 people died of asthma compared to 41 who died in a tornado. Let's try one more. Are people more likely to be killed in a homicide or kill themselves in a suicide? The media always covers homicides, but what about suicide? Statistics show that 12,000 people died of suicide compared to 9,200 who died in a homicide. This exercise demonstrates how we rely on heuristics to make judgments. We try to use all available information, but our information is often based on unsupported beliefs, rather than on hard data. In other words, we believe we have more knowledge than we actually do; we use what we have, and are confident that we are right.

Many times, heuristics or rules of thumb work quite well, but sometimes they are faulty. It's important to be aware that your knowledge, especially about the markets, may be limited. Groups of people may present you with information that a certain industry or sector is "hot" when, in fact, it's merely everyone erroneously believing the same inaccurate information. Be aware of this natural tendency to over-extend your knowledge and feel overconfident about decisions based on it. Question your knowledge. Get as much additional information as possible. Doing so will help you gain mastery over the tendency to act in an overconfident way.

Implications for Trading Performance

Online Trading Versus Brokers

Did you ever wonder if there were psychological implications from moving from phone-based investing with a broker to online investing? It appears that phone-based investing is correlated with overconfidence. In the "old days," there was a social interaction to think about when placing an order with a broker. For instance, the self-doubting trader may have thought, "I think I'll put off making this trade until I am convinced that my trading plan is absolutely going to produce a profit. I don't want my broker to think that I don't know what I'm doing." One may have also thought, "I'm going to hold on to this losing trade. I don't want to admit to my broker that I was wrong." Online investing eliminated these social interactions, but did it make a difference? A study by behavioral economists Drs. Barber and Odean (2000) suggests that it might have. They examined client statements from a large brokerage between January 1991 and December 1996. Investors who switched to online investing were compared to those who stayed with phone-based investing.

Investors who went online were more likely to be young men with high incomes and who had no children. They also reported that they had more trading experience and a preference for investing in small growth stocks with high market risk. Prior to investing online, they experienced unusually strong performance compared to investors who remained with phone-based investing. Switching to online investing clearly had an impact on trading patterns and performance. Investors who went online traded more actively than they had previously, but their trades were less profitable.

How can one explain these findings? Drs. Barber and Odean argue that online traders were "overconfident." They had experienced unusually good performance before switching to online trading, and this made them feel overconfident. Drs. Barber and Odean note that their findings are consistent with the social psychological literature on self-serving biases. Many people are "overconfident" in that they believe they have more knowledge than they actually do and believe they can control events more than they actually can (an illusion of control). A limitation of this study, however, is that overconfidence was not measured, and thus, one does not know with certainty that the online investors were actually overconfident. But these findings are thought provoking. Are we making more trades than we should merely because online trading has made executing a trade easier? Are we too overconfident in our abilities or knowledge? It is worth thinking about.

Rosy Glow Optimists Versus Defensive Pessimists

Many traders believe their problem is not having a winning attitude. Although a winning attitude is important, it's important not to let a winning attitude turn into overconfidence. Sometimes, it's useful to curb optimism. You may want to ask yourself, "Is being a pessimist all so bad?" Popular inspirational books, such as *The Power of Positive Thinking* (Peale, 1952) imply that optimism is "good" and pessimism is "bad." This view sometimes extends to professional psychology as well. For example, Dr. Martin Seligman (1990) argues in his book *Learned Optimism* that success is associated with optimism. Optimists are more likely to persist when faced with severe setbacks, while pessimists tend to give up easily, after only a minor setback. Dr. Seligman originally studied clinical depression, a chronic form of pessimism. It's his life mission to teach chronic pessimists to be optimists, and that is a noble endeavor. However, optimism may be a problem for traders, rather than an asset. Indeed, Dr. Terrance Odean (Gervais & Odean, 2001), a behavioral economist, argues that investors and traders are often too optimistic and too overconfident. They tend to take risks that they should not, ending up with lower amounts of capital than if they had been a little less optimistic. This controversy can't be resolved easily, but let's consider some scientific evidence that suggests that pessimism is not necessarily a bad thing.

Dr. Nancy Cantor and colleagues (Cantor, Norem, Niedenthal, Langston, & Brower, 1987) studied two groups of people they called the rosy glow optimists and the defensive pessimists. University of Michigan students were followed throughout the semester. At the start of the semester, participants were asked to predict their end-of-semester grades, and throughout the semester, they reported their emotions. Rosy glow optimists viewed academic tasks as challenging but not especially overwhelming. Defensive pessimists, in contrast, viewed academic tasks as difficult and as the cause of unpleasant stressful emotions. They believed that they would not achieve good grades unless they put in a lot of effort. They underestimated their performance, setting defensively low expectations despite stellar academic performance in previous semesters. Holding a pessimistic outlook seemed to prevent them from becoming overly confident and straying from their disciplined study schedule. Throughout the semester, defensive pessimists felt greater stress and anxiety than rosy glow optimists. Interestingly, this pessimistic outlook was not debilitating. In fact, among the pessimists, unpleasant emotions were correlated with higher grade point averages at the end of the semester. But overall, defensive pessimists did not differ from rosy glow optimists. That is, pessimism did not have an adverse influence on performance.

Under the right circumstances, and for certain people, pessimism is beneficial. Considering that several studies in behavioral finance have shown that traders tend to be overconfident, it may be useful to question one's confidence occasionally. Ask yourself, "Am I really certain that this trade is going to be successful or am I taking an unnecessary risk? Have I put in enough time and preparation into this trading plan?" It couldn't hurt to use a little caution. Sometimes, a little pessimism is not such a bad thing.

The Limitations of Positive Thinking

There is no doubt that positive thinking is "powerful." Successful people think positively. They believe that an optimistic attitude, combined with hard work and perseverance, will allow them to achieve any goal they attempt. However, let's take a contrary view for moment. Are there times when positive thinking can be a limitation rather than an asset? Psychologists have been studying when positive thinking can limit success rather than advance it.

Before discussing limitations of positive thinking, it's worth reviewing some of its advantages. Positive thinking is related to optimism. It's more advantageous to argue that the glass is half full than half empty. Obviously, without an optimistic attitude, we may never make a trade. It's vital for traders to believe that overall, after a series of well-planned trades, the equity in one's account will increase. If one were to believe it would decrease, he or she would never execute a trade. Positive thinking is especially useful when a person is feeling down and beaten. At these times, you need to pick yourself up by your bootstraps and put every bit of effort and energy you can muster into turning things around.

That said, let's now turn to the limitations of positive thinking. Positive thinking can sometimes produce unrealistic and inaccurate probability estimates. In one classic set of studies, participants were asked to make judgments as to the probability that specific favorable events will occur in a gambling situation. Specifically, people were asked to predict the probability that a particular outcome would occur during a successive series of "random" events. The events were not actually random, but were controlled by the researchers. Interestingly, people with an optimistic outlook were less accurate than people who were pessimistic, or even those prone to experience depression. This phenomenon has sometimes been referred to as "depressive realism" because the judgments of depressed or pessimistic people were more accurate than optimistic people. This well-established scientific finding highlights how many people are prone to hold beliefs that reflect "positive illusions" of control. That is, they believe that events are more controllable and predictable than they really are.

It's important to be aware of the tendency to be overly optimistic. In many professions it's useful to be optimistic. For example, if you are a salesperson trying to meet a sales quota, it isn't useful to believe that the quota cannot be met. It's fine to be overly optimistic and say, "I'm going to cold call as many people as I can to make those sales." One has to be a little more cautious when trading, however. It's useful to believe that one has a trading strategy that will give him or her an edge over a series of trades. But one doesn't need to be overly positive about it. A more neutral and somewhat skeptical approach may be more useful, such as thinking, "I believe this strategy will work, but I'm not absolutely certain that it will. I'll never know unless I try it, so I'm going to try it." The success or failure of the strategy need not carry any personal meaning. The success doesn't need to validate your ability as a trader or your worth as a person. To the extent that the outcome of a trade does not carry any personal significance, the better off one will be in the long run. Taking a more restrained optimistic approach will be more related to sound judgment, rather than an overly positive and almost euphoric approach.

Positive thinking used in moderation can be useful. But it's important to learn how to think both positively and realistically.

Unrealistic Optimism and Misperceptions of Risk

An on-going controversy among psychologists concerns the benefits of optimism. Some psychologists argue that optimism is always beneficial, while other psychologists point out that extreme levels of optimism may be associated with biased and inaccurate estimates of negative outcomes. There are clear advantages to holding an optimistic attitude. Rather than limit your success, it is useful to have a positive attitude, and believe that life offers endless opportunities for success. Why limit yourself by thinking that you will experience unfavorable events? Well...it depends on the accuracy of your perceptions.

A crucial distinction can be made between realistically estimating the probability of favorable events and unrealistically believing that favorable events will occur, when they are unlikely to occur. Realistic optimism is more useful than unrealistic optimism. For example, if you have a very poor trading strategy, it isn't realistic to believe that it will produce profits over a long series of trades. Unless one carefully and objectively monitors the success of a trading strategy, and determines its actual success, the equity in one's account can be rapidly depleted. A realistic estimate must be calculated and a new strategy must be developed should the estimate reveal the trading strategy is unprofitable. One may hold optimistic beliefs, but they must be accurate. Unrealistic optimism may lead to not only inaccurate estimates of failure, but inaction regarding necessary precautions to prevent such failure.

A recent study by Radcliffe and Klein (2002) illustrates the disadvantages of unrealistic optimism. Participants were asked to estimate the probability that they would experience an unfavorable outcome, in which an "objective" estimate of the actual probability was known. Unrealistic optimists underestimated the probability of the unfavorable event compared to realistic optimists. They also allowed their unrealistic optimism to influence their behavior. When presented with information regarding how they could reduce the probability of the unfavorable event, they did not review it closely, compared to realistic optimists. In addition, unrealistic optimists did not show proper concern and did not take necessary steps to move the probabilities in their favor.

These findings illustrate how optimism sometimes reflects a "defensive" motive to protect one's self-esteem. Rather than developing realistic expectations of an unfavorable event, and taking proper precautions to decrease the occurrence of the event, unrealistic optimists ignore important information that may signal a downfall.

Too much optimism is unrealistic, yet too little optimism can be very self-limiting. It's critical that you find the right balance between realistic self-motivating optimism and unrealistic biased optimism. Make sure that you are using optimistic beliefs to your advantage.

Thinking In Probabilities: A Critique

Many have espoused the virtue of "thinking in probabilities." It helps one maintain a positive mindset. Indeed, it promotes a positive mindset, but upon closer examination, this "thinking strategy" may also promote overconfidence. Perhaps, one of the most eloquent accounts of "thinking in probabilities" was written by Mark Douglas (2000) in his book, *Trading in the Zone*. Douglas suggests that traders should think like a professional gambler (pp. 101-106). Professional gamblers believe they have an "edge" and that if enough hands are played, they will come out a winner. Casinos, for example, build in an edge. They make sure a slot machine pays out less than it takes in. On any one pull, a gambler may win the jackpot, but over the course of a year, the casino comes out ahead. Traders can view trading the same way. Douglas says, "The trader's analytical tools are the known variables that put the odds of success (the edge) for any given trade in the trader's favor, in the same way that the rules of the game put the odds of success in favor of the casino."

It may be useful to use such a "thinking strategy," as Douglas puts it. Believing the odds are in your favor, if you play enough hands or make enough trades, will help you develop a carefree attitude toward trading. It will help you get "in the zone." But that's about it. As far as analogies go, it's dead wrong.

Douglas rightly notes, "Events that have probable outcomes can produce consistent results, if you get the odds in your favor and there is a large enough sample size." But from a purely statistical point of view, this statement has nothing to do with trading. Trading isn't like flipping a coin or playing Blackjack, in which cards are drawn from a deck of playing cards. In these instances, the statistical process is clear. In flipping a coin, there are only two possible outcomes, heads or tails. Playing cards also concerns a fixed set of outcomes. Mathematicians who work in the field of statistics run computer simulations to determine what the "sampling distribution" will look like should an event be repeated an infinite number of times. Flipping a coin or throwing a die, for example, can be approximated with the binomial distribution. Statisticians can use sampling distributions to make a probabilistic prediction of events. This cannot be done for trading strategies. Trading conditions are not consistent, whereas most games of chance, in theory, are consistent. Consistency allows for the mathematician to calculate the probability of an event. The trading context is different in another way: trading outcomes may be biased by a single factor, such as a long-term bear market that pushes prices down. Arriving at an accurate estimate of the odds of an event requires a set of conditions that are not present in the markets. The markets are too inconsistent, too unpredictable, and too chaotic. The professional gambling analogy just doesn't apply.

So when you think in terms of probabilities, realize it is merely a "thinking strategy." You are merely pretending that the odds are in your favor. You merely believe that with a "large sample" you will come out ahead. But also be aware that these are merely assumptions, which may produce an unwarranted sense of optimism. Don't let the technical jargon of statistics, which is a misuse of terms in this case, fool you into believing that the odds are in your favor. The odds may not be in your favor. No one really knows.

Watch Your Confidence Level

Self-confidence is an essential part of trading success. But confidence becomes lethal if it is not based on a solid track record or is overly influenced by emotional events; that is because successful traders are normally playing in, around, and off of what the market is doing without them. They try to make money by watching the trend and reacting quickly and intelligently. This, of course, takes confidence. But confidence sometimes grows into overconfidence. This can happen at the tail end of a winning streak, when euphoric events in your life make you feel omnipotent, or even when you begin to listen too closely to the admiration and appreciation that comes with financial success. The moment a trader develops too much confidence, he or she steps over the line between continuing success and dangerous brinkmanship. This can happen in a variety of ways. Consider some of the symptoms and consequences of overconfidence.

Taking too much risk: Successful traders take on risk that is manageable and in proportion to the potential reward. Overconfident traders often take on too much risk. This risk can be in the form of excessive position sizes, too much of their account balance riding on a single market factor, or allowing too much leeway for a trade that goes in the wrong direction.

Imposing your will onto the market: Successful traders allow the market to call the tune. They simply look for certain kinds of opportunities the market creates. They let the market take them where it goes, rather than believing they can control the markets. Overconfident traders believe they are above the market, or at least impervious to its power. They convince themselves the market will move their way, and rack up big-time losses waiting for their ideas and their trades to prevail. They usually wait so long they wind up taking a fall.

Need to be right: Successful traders cautiously try to account for all possibilities before they pull the trigger. They develop detailed trading plans and are quick to get out if their calculations and expectations do not immediately pan out. Overconfident traders are too certain of their own correctness. They allow their expectations to overpower their analyses. They are more willing to bet the bundle on long-shot opportunities. As a result, they often stay in the high-risk game long enough for the odds to stack up against them.

Watch your confidence level. Make sure you maintain an appropriate level of confidence. Look out for the signs and symptoms of overconfidence, and ensure that overconfidence does not get the best of you.

Moving Full Speed Ahead

Confidence in your knowledge, skills, and preparation are the foundation of a winning state of mind. However, events or experiences in your personal life may affect that confidence.

When events and experiences negatively influence a trader's confidence, chances are that at some level, he or she is aware of the influence and also realizes that it's very difficult to overcome it in a timely manner. He or she forms a "pseudo-confident" mental state to replace what should be true confidence, because he or she knows that confidence is the precursor to success. But that confidence must be real, rather than a form of "pseudo-confidence." Pseudo-confidence arises when traders wrongly believe their inaccurate knowledge is accurate or that they possess trading skills that they have not yet attained.

Symptoms of a pseudo-confident mental approach are making decisions very quickly, not pausing to evaluate or reflect on activity before the next decision, excusing losses as a part of what needs to be done to be successful, and not objectively evaluating them.

Pseudo-confidence makes the trader especially vulnerable to giving into emotions like fear and greed without even realizing it. It's part of a process where traders deny weaknesses, believing they are easy to overcome and that all one needs to do is move full speed ahead. But doing so will lead one to inevitably err. The pseudo-confident approach doesn't allow the trader to really evaluate any decision he or she is making. And with the slightest influence of emotions, the trader will consistently make losing decisions.

Are you truly confident? Are you "creating" confidence because you know you need it? It's very important for a trader to be self-aware. Asking such questions can provide insight. Clearly though, it's not enough to simply ask the questions. You have to be objective in your answers and work to resolve the underlying issues.

If your personal life has a way of working itself into your trading life, you need to stop and consider why that's happening. Look to your knowledge, skills, and trading plans to guide you to a more protected trading approach that is hard to influence through your environment.

Forward Opportunities

What was the last thing you traded? Look at its 1-year, 6-month, 1-month, and 3-5 day charts. Can you see all the opportunities where you could have made a profit? Should have gone long there, shorted here... You're assessing "opportunity" based on price activity subsequent to the point at which you believe the opportunity existed, which means that you're working backward to identify that point of opportunity.

While trading, these are the very opportunities a trader tries to spot. This and the desire to make trades will often drive the inexperienced trader to "see" opportunity where there is none, simply because the trader can easily envision the price pattern moving in any given direction. If his or her predisposition or any of his or her analysis makes him or her inclined to forecast a certain direction, he or she can quickly envision the movement of price in the direction that will yield profits. By envisioning such price pattern formations, it's often the case that the trader will mentally emulate what he or she has previously viewed on historical charts, and perhaps even had a desire to experience. And this psychology is made even more complex when the trader begins to find "evidence" in current price activity that supports his or her forecast/vision and ignores any information that contradicts it, thereby providing a false justification to make the trade.

This type of thinking will cause a trader to make trades when no real opportunity exists. The fundamental problem is that the reason for action is based on a forecast/vision, and not on what has happened and what is happening right now. Given the fact that forecasts and visions are not realities, yet historical and current activities are realities, decisions that are based on the proper interpretation of what has happened and is happening will be correct far more often. It's critical to avoid mentally creating opportunities and to know when to stay out of a trade.

Looking at the charts again, try to identify forward-looking opportunities, where you consider only each price point and the price patterns before it. You'll find that it's now far more difficult to spot the winners, but those are the opportunities that you need to identify and then appropriately act on in order to be a successful trader.

Any experienced and successful trader will agree that it's very important not to trade until there's a true opportunity.

The Gambler's Fallacy: A Critique

Have you heard about the gambler's fallacy? Have you been warned to avoid it? Many trading books cover the gambler's fallacy (for example, see Tharp, 1999, p. 38). It's worth a more in-depth look and critique. Here's a demonstration, if you haven't seen it already. A coin is tossed 10 times. Consider two possible outcomes of 10 tosses where H is <u>heads</u> and T is <u>tails</u>.

A. HHHHHHHHHH
B. HHTHTHTHTH

If you need to get a tails on the next toss (to win a bet, for example), which sequence would you prefer, A or B? Most people choose A. Why? People think, "There is a 50-50 chance of getting heads on any one toss, so after the string of heads in sequence A, the next toss is bound to result in a tails." There is a very human tendency to believe that there is equilibrium when it comes to probability. When one event seems to occur "more than it is supposed to by chance," events should work out so that the 50-50 chance is restored. But the fallacy is to forget, or to not know, about the theoretical probability of flipping a coin. What does a "50-50 chance" mean? We use this phrase often in common language, but we often misunderstand its meaning. Here's the formal definition. If a coin were tossed an infinite number of times, 50% of the outcomes would be heads and 50% of the outcomes would be tails. Thus, the "expected outcome" on any one toss would be 50% heads and 50% tails. The key word is "expected outcome." That's a term that statisticians use in probability theory to talk about hypothetical outcomes in hypothetical, or ideal, situations. When one talks of tossing a coin an infinite number of times (which can't be done), then one can talk about the hypothetical outcome as a 50-50 chance of getting heads on the next toss, for example.

The gambler's fallacy is merely an intellectual question: Do you know about probability and how to estimate the odds? When you toss a coin an infinite number of times, sequence A or sequence B is equally likely, so one is equally likely to get a tails on the next toss with either sequence. So if you picked A, you were wrong in terms of the academic study of probability and statistics. But what does any of this have to do with trading?

It's funny that this issue is even brought up when it comes to trading. Trading methods are not like flipping a coin. Probability theory is often misused in trading. Probability theory only applies to a process with known outcomes that can be repeated an infinite number of times under the *same* conditions. Trading methods don't have known outcomes (back testing only offers an estimate of how well the method did in the past; descriptive statistics can be used but not inferential statistics; Murphy, 1999), and market conditions are always changing. So probability theory doesn't apply.

The truth is, in theory, a string of losing trades with the same method could mean that the next trade will be a loser because of market conditions alone. (That said, don't believe, however, that a string of losses means it's time for you to have a winner because the events need to "equal out" due to chance. That's a misunderstanding of probability.) The main lesson to learn is to not be fooled into thinking that trading is more "scientific" than it really is. Professionally trained statisticians are not doing scientific studies of a trading method and arriving at what a real statistician would call the probability of success. When you hear such claims, see them for what they are. It's just a belief. If a trading method worked 75% on historical data, one may claim that it will work 75% in the future. Well, maybe. A statistician would say such a statement is merely wishful thinking, and clearly a misuse of probability theory. Don't be fooled. Trading outcomes can't be predicted with any amount of certainty. There is strength in knowledge. Knowing that no one can estimate the odds of a strategy working in the future will give you an edge.

Taking Responsibility

Successful traders take responsibility for their actions. They believe their success is due to their well-developed skills and persistent effort, rather than a matter of circumstance, luck, or chance. Psychologists call this tendency an internal locus of control. Several scientific studies have shown that taking responsibility for one's actions is related to success (internal), while making excuses or avoiding responsibility is associated with failure (external). A study by Dr. Peter Chui (2001), however, suggests there may be a downside to taking too much responsibility.

A common tendency among traders is to sell off winning investments too soon while holding on to losing investments too long. This tendency has been replicated in several scientific field studies of investors and experiments with college students. One explanation for this tendency is that upon seeing a profit on a trade, investors want to "lock in" their profits, and thus, they close out the trade before the price moves against them. Often, the investor would have realized greater profits if he or she could have held the trade a little longer. Investors hold on to a losing trade on the chance that the price will move in their favor if they wait long enough. This strategy often results in even greater losses.

Traders may differ on the tendency to liquidate winning trades prematurely, while holding losing trades too long. Dr. Chui was interested in whether some people are more likely to show this tendency than others. In his study, college students were allowed to invest in six stocks in a simulation task. Participants were given an actual amount of money to trade, so that the simulation was closer to "real life" in that losses were associated with disappointment and winnings were associated with elation. In a series of trades across 14 time periods, participants were allowed to buy, sell, or hold stocks, but were required to sell all stocks at the end of simulation. As expected, participants tended to liquidate winning trades prematurely, while holding on to losing trades too long. This finding was consistent with several previous studies.

A novel aspect of Dr. Chui's study is that he measured participants' tendency to take responsibility for their trading outcomes, rather than attributing them to luck or chance. He discovered that participants who attribute trading outcomes to luck or chance are less likely to sell winning trades prematurely or to hold on to losing trades too long. Dr. Chui offers a psychological explanation for his findings. People who do not believe their results are due to their own actions have little need to defend themselves psychologically against failure, and are not afraid to seek out risk. People who take full responsibility, in contrast, may be over-concerned with failure and take efforts to prevent it by closing winning positions early to ensure a win.

Dr. Chui argues that traders may not be aware of how often they are afraid to take risks, and thus, may be missing opportunities to increase their overall profits. The lesson to learn from Dr. Chui's findings is that it is necessary to take the appropriate amount of responsibility for your success. Certainly, it is not a good idea to make excuses or avoid responsibility, but taking too much responsibility is not a good idea either. When you believe that all of your success as a trader is due to your ability and talent, you may be putting your self-esteem and identity on the line with each trade. Finding the right balance between taking appropriate responsibility and placing blame elsewhere is a challenge that all traders must learn to meet.

Overtrading

As the term implies, overtrading is the tendency to put on trades unnecessarily. Behavioral economists and trading coaches propose various reasons for overtrading. Some traders merely believe, "a real trader trades all day," while other traders may crave the excitement that excessive trading brings. Still others may overtrade to cope with a general frustration they feel in their lives. For them, putting on trades is like playing the lottery: every trade brings hope of success and fulfillment. Others are just plain greedy and hope to make as much profit as possible during the trading day. Overtrading doesn't usually pay off, however, as shown by Drs. Barber and Odean (2000), in what has now become a classic study in behavioral finance.

Barber and Odean studied trading patterns at a large brokerage. They identified overtraders based on the number of trades they made and examined the amount of profits each group realized over the course of a year. They wanted to see whether overtraders could beat investors who used a simple buy-and-hold strategy, which is a relatively conservative trading strategy. Average annual turnover was 250% for overtraders and 2.4% for buy-and-hold investors. Surprisingly, both groups achieved an 18.7% gross return on their investments, but the net return differed greatly. Due to commissions, the overtrading group's net return was 11.4% while the buy-and-hold group's net return was 18.5%. It's also useful to note that the buy-and-hold investors also benefited from lower capital gains taxes by holding investments for a year.

Barber and Odean's study was conducted with long-term investors, but what are the implications for traders? If a trader is using a traditional broker that charges a large commission for a round trip trade, then it is quite relevant. Overtrading costs a great deal in commissions and fees and in capital gains taxes. And even someone using a discount broker who charges a few dollars per trade, still pays capital gains taxes. Thus, it is vital that one identify high probability trades; follow the old adage: for every dollar you risk, make sure your trading strategy will pay out three dollars.

Besides commission costs, it's useful to consider that overtrading, especially among traders, may reflect psychological issues that should be addressed and resolved. Behavioral economists attribute overtrading to the tendency to be overconfident. People over extend their knowledge: they believe they have more knowledge of price than they possibly can and believe they have more control than they actually do. If you are prone to this tendency, it's a good idea to curb it before it costs you a lot of money. Don't feel that it is necessary to make a lot of trades to be a successful trader. For many, the more trades you make, the more money you will lose overall.

Curbing Your Overconfidence

Don't Get High On Your Success

The trading world is full of stories about tremendous success, and most trading coaches hold out the promise of unlimited success if only you'll follow their advice (and not incidentally, pay for their services). But it's also important to learn how to handle success when it comes your way. How you handle success reveals a great deal about your chances of hanging on to that level of success for any important length of time.

The truth is that a good many traders who achieve significant success suffer a kind of "psychological fallout" that not only hurts themselves, but their loved ones and others around them. And it should be no surprise that one of the most common reactions to such enormous success is, of course, to give all or most of it back to the market.

In fact, there are many traders who believe you will not be able to make and hang onto significant success in the markets unless you are prepared to handle big money and high levels of freedom and power. Here are a few preventative strategies that can be taken to help you manage your trading success.

Focus on the markets, not the money: As your success increases, your position sizes and a typical day's winnings tend to become outsized. Earning a car or a house in a single day can throw you off balance emotionally. To prevent this, work to get your satisfaction from following your trading method more closely, rather than from trading larger amounts. Feel a sense of reward and satisfaction when you stick with your trading plan. It's also vital to view your profits as a percentage of your account balance, rather than raw dollars.

Establishing a lifestyle you can afford: Trading with the rent money is a sure way to increase your stress levels and decrease your chances of success. It's important to "only trade money you can afford to lose." By keeping your expenses to a minimum, you can follow this adage. As you become more successful, apply some of your surplus toward a sustainable lifestyle that is independent of future trading income. By isolating your family's basic living expenses from your day-to-day trading results, you make it easier to stay loose and in tune with the markets.

Feeling comfortable with the envy of others: Big-time trading success will almost always attract a certain amount of attention, especially if you change your lifestyle drastically. It's a powerful moment when you make more in a week or month than your parents earned in a year or a lifetime. If you let your head swell from all this, you'll almost certainly lose that delicate balance between a big ego and the humility that keeps top traders in close touch with the markets.

You Are Brilliant

You often hear stories about successful traders who've taken very large losses and bounced back to experience even greater success. Losing a third or even half of your trading capital can be devastating, even for the best and experienced traders, at least that's what a trader without a winning attitude would expect. But one rarely hears successful traders say, "I don't think I can come back" or "That's it for me, I'm out." In fact, if they did say that, it's hard to see how they could have ever been successful traders in the first place. And it's not the fact that the trader gets over his or her losses that he or she is able to come back. The successful trader doesn't even perceive the losses as something to "get over." Winning attitudes help traders stay positive.

Self-confidence, determination, and persistence exemplify the trader with the winning attitude. Such traders truly believe they are brilliant traders. When they take a loss here and there, and even when they take a loss large enough to cause other traders to reconsider their chosen career, their resolve is unshaken. Their self-confidence and belief in their brilliance as a trader is as untarnished as it is on his biggest winning day. It's because their self-confidence is based on solid performance records.

There are few traders with truly solid self-confidence; they're the ones who are most experienced and successful over a long period of time. It's easy to mimic having a winning attitude while you're on a winning streak - you'd be surprised at the number of traders who do this. They don't truly have solid self-confidence. Their unfounded self-confidence is merely overconfidence. They hope they will be successful, although they have yet to develop the requisite skills.

As a trader, it's important to nurture your winning attitude and develop it to its full potential. But it's vital that this winning attitude is based on solid information, rather than wishful thinking. When a winning attitude reflects true self-confidence based on a solid trading record, it's an asset. The best way to do this is through continuous self-assessment and evaluation, especially in terms of your trading activity. Ruthlessly monitor your thoughts, feelings, and actions. Be open-minded. Accept your true nature. By developing a valid winning attitude, you will defeat overconfidence and act out of a true sense of self-confidence.

Self-efficacy: The Antidote for Overconfidence

One of the biggest psychological issues traders face is overconfidence. Overconfidence is not the same thing as self-esteem. Self-esteem is a personality trait that develops over time and applies to a wide range of situations. People with either high or low self-esteem can be prone to overconfidence. Behavioral economists define overconfidence as the tendency to believe one has more trading skills than he or she actually has. The markets are hard to understand and predict. To cope with this ambiguity, traders believe they have more information than they really have and believe their trading strategies are more effective than they really are. People with high self-esteem are overconfident because they are used to being successful, and may believe their previous success in one area, such as occupational or school success, can apply directly to trading. People with low self-esteem are often anxious and intimidated by the markets and are overconfident so as to relieve anxiety and fear: it's like saying, "Maybe if I pretend to know what I'm doing, I'll feel more self-assured." It's dangerous to be overconfident. One may risk money on trades prematurely, before one has all the facts or a well-defined trading plan.

The best antidote to overconfidence is to break down the trading process into specific steps and study each step closely. It's also important to gauge self-efficacy and increase it, when it is low. Self-efficacy, proposed by Dr. Albert Bandura (1977), is sometimes called situational confidence (Reilly et al., 1995). One may have high self-esteem in that he or she feels confident in many areas of life, but may not feel very confident in a particular situation, such as during different phases of trading. A process, such as trading, can be broken down into component parts, and people can vary on how confident they feel while executing each part. For example, putting on a trade can be broken down into a set of events: plan an entrance and exit strategy (stop loss or exit point, etc.), read the market (accurately perceiving an opportunity, determining momentum), enter the market (trade execution), monitor the price action, and exit at the right time. It's possible to feel confident at one or more of these steps but not at others; for example, one can know how to execute a trade and exit, but not know how to determine momentum accurately. How much confidence or self-efficacy do you have regarding each of these steps or trading situations? It probably depends on your performance. If you feel you can perform the task well, you feel very confident. If you feel you cannot, you feel less confident. It's important to have an accurate assessment of your abilities. Then, it's also vital that you set realistic goals and practice to achieve them. Research studies have shown that the more self-efficacy one develops, the higher level of performance one achieves. The iterative process of realistically assessing performance, practicing to achieve higher levels, and building greater levels of self-efficacy based on new levels of performance is the most effective way to achieve a higher level of performance and trade more effectively. Rather than be overconfident and trade on the abilities you don't have, it is vital to beat the problem of overconfidence by accurately assessing your skills and practicing to reach new levels of performance.

Chapter 4

Motivation and Personality

In the field of psychology, the study of motivation and personality is one of the most controversial areas. As non-psychologists, we know that our friends and loved ones differ in terms of personality traits and the conscious and unconscious motives that underlie their behavior, but psychologists remain skeptical and undecided as to whether these factors are of any significant consequence. For example, social psychologists have traditionally argued that situations control behavior, and that motives and personality are of little consequence. Similarly, cognitive psychologists and behavioral economists argue that decision-making biases are manifested by all investors and traders, regardless of their motives or personality.

Trading situations may provoke anxiety and stress, but are there individual differences? Are all people naturally inclined to respond with stress, or are some people more anxiety-prone or stress-prone than others? Most trading and investment psychology books suggest that seasoned traders have an ideal personality style. For example, an individual with high levels of risk tolerance, emotion control, self-esteem, and logical reasoning ability would be a more effective trader than an individual who is low on these personality traits. But it's not clear that one is doomed to failure if he or she fears risks, is over-emotional, or intuitive. One can develop strategies to work around one's personality. This person versus situation controversy cannot be resolved here, but the general issue is addressed: What is the ideal trader personality type? What can I change? For which traits must I compensate? The key is to assess one's personality, gain awareness of it, and try to compensate for it. This chapter consists of a set of essays that illustrate how this can be done.

The second half of the chapter covers motivation. Motives can be unconscious or conscious. That is, one may struggle to satisfy unconscious basic needs of sex and aggression or consciously strive for fulfillment and self-actualization. Psychological motives are tantamount for long-term success as a trader. It's possible to achieve phenomenal short-term success, yet fail miserably in the long term because unconscious motives and needs are left unmet. Understanding what motivates you as a trader, identifying unresolved psychological conflicts, and cultivating your creative side can help you enhance your performance and remain profitable over the long term.

The Ideal Trading Personality

Walking the Tightrope

A popular prototype of a supertrader is someone who can take risks and think independently, yet has extreme self-control and discipline to stick to one's trading plan. Although in an intellectual sense it's possible to imagine such a person, such people are quite rare. There's a difference between myth and reality. Personality traits tend to go together or "correlate" with each other in a consistent overall pattern, which means that some personality types are more likely to exist among people than others. Independent thinkers tend to be risk takers, yet tend to lack self-discipline. In contrast, people who have self-control and discipline tend to be conformists who avoid risk. Thus, the ideal supertrader personality type is quite rare, and reflects myth and legend more than reality.

There's no sense in trying to become a "type" of person who may not exist. To be successful as a trader, it's vital that you learn where you stand on conformity, discipline, and risk aversion, monitor your behaviors, and work with the personality you have. Compare yourself to the ideal prototype of the supertrader to determine where you stand on each trait, and control the "negative" traits that work against you as a trader. It is much like walking a tightrope between two extremes. For example, non-conforming independent thinkers must control their impulses and try to maintain discipline. These individuals must learn to follow rules and stick to them, when it's appropriate. They need to prevent themselves from putting on trades to get a quick thrill. But they can't take it too far, and be overcontrolled and risk averse. This is harder to do than it sounds, since it's hard to fight against your natural inclination. For example, it's hard for people who are risk takers to see themselves that way, identify this tendency as a "problem," and learn to control it.

Although "conformity" is viewed as "bad" in trading books, successful people are conformists. Conformists, who usually have little problems with self-control and discipline, must be careful not to be too rule-orientated. Highly successful people have the ability to examine social situations, extract subtle social rules, and change their behavior accordingly. Such perceptiveness and self-control are the hallmarks of success. But these traits can be problematic for trading if the individual tries to impose rules and structure onto the markets, since universal rules don't apply. The markets are less predictable than the events usually encountered in everyday life. For conforming individuals, it's useful to cultivate one's more impulsive and intuitive side, and try to take some risks. But again, it's important to find the right balance between extreme discipline and impulsiveness.

In the end, it's impossible to strive to become and adhere to a personality style that only exists in the trading folklore. Although in a philosophical sense, we can all imagine a person who thinks independently, takes risks, and yet shows extreme discipline; few people show the right "mix" of these personality traits. The best we can do is identify where we stand on each of these traits, recognize that our trading behaviors may be limited by these traits, and develop a method that works around our personality.

Risk Taking versus Risk Seeking

Prominent business leaders often portray themselves as risk takers. The business literature is replete with anecdotes of entrepreneurs who put it all on the line, took a big risk, and made a big win. There is some evidence, however, that successful entrepreneurs and traders are not risk takers at all. Indeed, those who are successful in business are more likely to avoid risk rather than seek it out.

A dictionary definition of risk is "a course of action that involves danger or hazard." To some extent, anyone who makes a trade is taking a risk in that it is possible that a great deal of the money can be lost. This loss is a danger or hazard. Risk takers can be distinguished from risk seekers, however. A risk taker is someone who exposes himself or herself to a risk, such as when a person makes a trade. A risk seeker, in contrast, is a person who likes risk, seeks it out, and enjoys the thrill of taking a risk. A risk taker does not necessarily need to be a risk seeker.

Successful traders may be willing to take a risk, but they don't seek them out. They are not gamblers who enjoy the thrill of the possibility that they may lose a great deal of money. Instead, they take a calculated risk. They minimize the amount of risk on any single trade and look at the potential downside. They consider the possibility that one may face a series of losing trades and that, should this happen, they ensure they have enough equity in their account to make it through this run of bad luck. By risking only a relatively small amount of equity on any single trade, they protect their equity should they face several losing trades.

In contrast, risk seekers are people who do not look at the consequences of their actions. Risk seekers often act impulsively and approach each trade as potentially the one big trade that may set them up for life. The risk seeker is ready to make a big bet, while the successful trader may be willing to take a risk, but not that much of a risk.

Successful traders also have different expectations regarding how the equity in their account increases. Risk seekers hope that their equity will increase rapidly, but successful traders are willing to let their equity increase in a slow steady linear fashion. They know that success comes in small steps. Risk seekers' equity tends to increase and decrease in a jagged pattern, and usually ends up as an overall decrease.

When you are trading, don't take unnecessary risks. Remember, successful traders may be risk takers, in that they are willing to lose a small amount of money, but they are not risk seekers. They want to limit their losses on any single trade, make a slow but steady profit, and patiently wait for their equity to increase.

Risk Tolerance

Risk tolerance is influenced by both personality and situational factors. People who are extreme perfectionists tend to be overly anxious and have the biggest problems with risk tolerance. They tend to ruminate about the worst-case scenario. They unrealistically believe that they will lose all their trading capital on a single trade. It's important to determine whether one falls into this category. If you have a problem with perfectionism or anxiety, it's important to examine the maladaptive beliefs that underlie these traits and change them.

Risk tolerance is also influenced by situational factors. If you have a problem with risk tolerance, you may want to consider changing some of these situational factors. For example, one may try to risk large positions to make a substantial profit. Although one must risk a large percentage of capital to make a substantial return, doing so causes stress and anxiety. If you are the kind of person who has a problem with stress and anxiety, it may be difficult to trade such large positions. One of the biggest mistakes people make when trying to cope with anxiety is doing too much too quickly. Don't start off trading larger positions until you have mastered trading smaller positions. Start with a small position, in which you can trade in a calm and relaxed manner. Once you have mastered that position size, gradually increase it, as if you are walking up a staircase one step at a time. If a larger size produces anxiety, move down one step and start over. Risk tolerance is something you can learn to master gradually over time.

Other situational factors that you can change to help gain a feeling of risk tolerance include placing a stop loss order to limit your risk or reducing the amount of time you hold a position. Some people have difficulty holding positions over a longer timeframe. This may be something you have to work up to. Again, increase the amount of time you hold a position in an incremental process, taking it one step at a time. You may also want to consider reducing your objectives. Rather than trying to make $5,000 a year, set your goal at $2,000 a year, for example. Doing so will reduce your stress level and increase your risk tolerance.

By changing both the personality and situational factors that underlie feelings of fear and anxiety, you can increase your risk tolerance. Situational factors are easier to change than personality factors, but making a change in either domain will increase your risk tolerance.

Out of Control

"I'm out of control" is the signature line from Dana Carvey's imitation of Regis Philbin. Regis has never said the line, but it seems consistent with his personality, according to "Live" producer Michael Gelman. Regis is a likable guy, but he acts a little over-excited at times. He is a little on-edge, as if he is ready to burst and lose control. Traders often talk about losing control, or trying to maintain control and discipline. When your money is on the line and the market prices are zigzagging up and down, it's easy to feel over-excited, a little on edge, and feel as if you might break down and have an "anxiety attack." Why do people lose control and how can traders maintain control? Some people have personality styles that may precipitate a loss of control. Here are some of the most common ones:

Impulsive personality: The impulsive personality is exemplified by the "gambler's instinct." These individuals like a thrill and are always trying to seek out excitement. Some scientists speculate that a genetic influence underlies impulsive personality, but it's mostly psychological. Impulsive persons often have trouble becoming self-sufficient and finding a true meaning around which to organize their lives. They are often bored and try to find thrills to ease the boredom. Compulsive- or problem-gamblers often have an impulsive personality. Such individuals may also be attracted to trading and it is important to make sure that you are not one of them. They love the thrill and excitement of putting on a trade. At an extreme, impulsive persons may not trade very consistently. They are often tempted to put on trades, even in low probability trading opportunities. That's not to say that impulsive people cannot be good traders. It's possible that they can make money in the short term, but they have trouble maintaining long-term success. That said, having a little bit of an impulsive side is useful for trading. In the end, one cannot be afraid to take a risk, and people who are a little bit impulsive can do so more easily than people who are exacting and over-controlled.

Anxious and fearful personality: Some people become fearful easily. When they experience fear, they lose control. They expend all their psychological resources combating anxiety and have little energy left to monitor their trades and maintain discipline. They often execute a trade too late and close out a trade too early. If one has an anxious personality, the easiest way to maintain control is to minimize risk. One should only trade money that he or she can afford to lose. Minimize the amount of money you risk on each trade and have well-defined exit strategies.

The perfectionist: Some people not only get anxious easily, but also are extreme perfectionists. They prefer to trade only a "sure thing" and fruitlessly try to find as much information about a trade as possible. They analyze and over-analyze and often fall prey to "analysis-paralysis." Ironically, this need for over-control often leads to under-control. Perfectionists are easily frustrated in uncertain situations, especially trading, which is very unpredictable and uncertain. When easily frustrated, perfectionists often make decisions out of desperation: they just want the uneasy feeling of confusion and uncertainty to end. They get in too late and get out too early, just to get the decision-making phase of trading over with.

Does one of these personality styles fit you? It's not an exhaustive list, and you may fit into more than one of the categories, but it's useful to find out what your trading personality is, and if you need to, find a way to change or compensate for your personality.

The Herd Mentality

Have you ever watched a herd of cattle as they graze in an open field? It's quite remarkable. The cows seem content as they eat the grass and stand in a scattered formation. Then, suddenly, for no apparent reason, one cow decides it has eaten enough, turns toward the barn and starts walking. The rest of the cows seem to follow, one by one, until the entire herd is moving in a straight line toward the barn. It is as if the cows are thinking, "Where's that guy going? What's he going after? I want to get in on this action. I'm going to follow him." They follow the leader even though the leader does not seem to know what it is doing. That's an extreme example of the herd mentality that some market observers see as analogous to the markets. One person starts buying, then another person, and so on, and so on, until a group of traders are all buying, for no apparent reason. Although humans have more intelligence than cattle, there is an inherent instinct to follow the crowd. It's as if everyone is thinking, "All of these people can't be wrong."

It makes sense to follow the crowd sometimes. In a bull market, prices continue to rise, so it makes sense to buy and hold. But when market conditions change, you better be careful to not let the traders in the back of the herd trample you when you try to stop so as to avoid hitting a brick wall. The crowd is usually right, until a turning point occurs. Why? When virtually everyone has taken the position that the market is headed in a particular direction, there are few traders left to push the trend further. At that point, a countertrend initiates and moves the market in the opposite direction (Pring, 1993). The trick is predicting when that turning point will occur, anticipating it, and developing a trading plan to capitalize on it. In the *Art of Contrary Thinking*, Humphrey Neill (cited in Pring, 1993) discusses how to take a contrary opinion. Taking a contrary opinion is not merely doing the opposite of what everyone else is doing. A true contrarian creatively studies the markets and tries to devise an innovative trading plan. It takes a great deal of experience and thought. One must train his or her mind to think in directions that are opposite to prevailing opinions. It's sort of like thinking in reverse. Think of reasons why the crowd may be wrong. Try to discover factors that may predict a change in market conditions, or identify new sectors that may prosper from the change. For example, during the great depression, consumers tended to stay home and listen to the radio, rather than go out to see movies or shows. Thus, radio companies made profits in a time of economic scarcity. A contrarian identifies such opportunities and capitalizes on them.

Taking a contrarian approach is useful, but it's often hard to fight the herd instinct. While trading, people have a natural inclination to see what everyone else is doing, and to follow. It feels safe and comfortable. But if one is not careful, following the crowd can lead to disaster. The crowd can be wrong. So always think like a contrarian. Study the markets carefully. Consider why the crowd may be wrong. Search for evidence that supports the contrarian position. If you are right, you can capitalize on it, and make a big win.

Changing Your Personality to Suit Your Trading Lifestyle

Many successful traders have entered trading after a successful career in another field. However, achieving success in the markets is quite different from achieving success in other occupations. The markets do not necessarily reward the personality traits that are developed and rewarded in other occupations. Do you have personality characteristics that got you ahead in your previous profession, but may not get you ahead in the markets? If you do, you may have to work on changing some of these traits to be a successful trader.

Let's review some of the personality traits that may not be conducive to trading. Take conformity, for example. When working your way up the corporate ladder, it's vital to be able to perceive how you fit into the organization. One must accurately perceive what his or her superiors view as the direction for the company, regardless of whether one agrees with this direction or not. Conformity is often rewarded over independent thinking and independence. If you have worked in a corporate setting, you are probably aware of how everyone seems to dislike the person who is always questioning group decisions and seems to self-promote his or her own ideas at the expense of the group. In contrast, conformity is a limitation rather than an asset when it comes to trading. Ideally, traders look only within themselves for the ultimate answers. They don't rely on the opinions of others, are skeptical of prevailing opinions, and continuously try to find a new trading plan before everyone else, so they can beat the crowd, rather than follow them.

Related to conformity is sociability. In many occupations, people work with other people. They must get along with others, perceive their needs, and sometimes yield to the needs of others at the expense of their own needs. Successful traders, in contrast, are rugged individualists. Many times, sociability and trading do not mix. A trader must make independent decisions, which again, means looking within themselves to find the right answers. It may also mean spending a great deal of time alone studying the markets and preparing for trades, rather than spending time with other people (which is also true of some other occupations). Traders must find the right balance between fulfilling the need for social contact and finding the time to spend alone to focus on one's trading passion.

Traders are creative people who take personal risks, think independently, and intensely focus on trading problems to develop innovative solutions. Creativity requires independent thinking, non-conformity, and social isolation. In many occupations, such traits are not viewed as desirable, so you may not have developed these traits. But if you trade full time, it is useful to develop some of these traits to some extent. You don't have to drastically change your personality, but be aware that some of the traits that precipitate success in other occupations don't get you ahead as a trader.

Motivation and Drive

What Motivates Your Trading?

An important aspect of your personality is the values that motivate you. Why do you trade? What are the reasons that you trade?

If you're trading for the wrong reasons, don't expect the same kind of positive results that so many top traders have achieved. To obtain the winning results, you must have the winning psychology, and that includes the kind of motivations that will induce you to trade prudently, effectively, and successfully.

Let's examine a few motivations and their likely impact on your trading results.

Excitement seeking: There's plenty of excitement when you have open positions in a fast moving market. But if you're too heavily motivated by the excitement alone, you probably won't trade well. Traders who seek out the excitement tend to take big risks trying for big wins, but they often chalk up big losses, instead. Giving in to a strong craving for excitement makes it difficult to maintain a high level of success for a long period of time.

Independence: Traders are among the purest entrepreneurs on the planet. They can generate huge gains without customers, assistants, expensive equipment, or heavy expenses. In fact, a desire for independence can help traders because it drives them to make their own trades, while everyone else follows the prevailing wisdom.

Quick riches: Newspaper, magazine, radio, and TV discussions of trading nearly always focus on the "get rich quick" angle. But while that's a distinct possibility, far more often a trader gets rich overnight only after having put in years and years of preparation, learning, and hard work. Traders who are motivated by the dream of instant wealth normally ignore proper risk management, allowing a losing streak to take them permanently out of the game.

Freedom: It's true that traders can work when and where they want. If you're motivated to trade by the thought of short hours and easy work days, you may be able to achieve what you're after. But success in trading can also depend on staying in tune with the markets, and that can require a heavy commitment over a long period of time. Striving for freedom is a double-edged sword: it's desirable, but usually requires a lot of extra work to achieve it.

Big paydays: Everyone has heard of traders earning five, six, even seven figures or more in a single day. But that's not the usual reward for newcomers. You must usually earn those big paydays through years of hard work, learning the markets, taking losses, and developing the nose and the reflexes to sniff opportunities and jump on them quickly. If you're motivated primarily by a desire to find the pot of gold at the end of the rainbow, you may find that trading puts a cloud in your future.

The challenge: The markets are a fascinating amalgam of the hopes and fears of millions of living human beings. The endless gyrations of individual prices provide a continuing challenge for traders who want to predict the future and capitalize on it. If you're motivated by this challenge, you will likely find nothing more satisfying than trading.

What Drives You?

Trading is a demanding profession, which makes success a lot more elusive for those with the wrong motivation. For those who learn how to trade successfully, of course, there is the promise of a large income, along with extremely flexible working hours and the ability to work from home. Yet anyone who pursues this career direction just for these benefits has a good chance of being disappointed. Experience shows, and the top traders tend to demonstrate, that success tends to settle on those who become serious, active traders for reasons of personal satisfaction.

Here is a checklist to see what is driving you along your path toward becoming a successful trader:

I like the process: Central to success as a trader is a genuine affection and appreciation for the daily grind that is involved. This includes the long hours, weeks, and months of study necessary to come up to speed, as well as the specific preparation for each workday. It also includes the constant uncertainty of trading, the frequent mistakes and surprises, and the steady evolution of the markets. If you are not happy dealing with situations like these, you are not cut out to be a trader.

I like the action: Physicians work with blood and organs to cure disease. Accountants are obsessed about very precise sums. Lawyers regularly dive into legal precedents to win a case. Traders must excel at decision-making under conditions of ambiguity and rapidly changing conditions. If you do not like the pressure of having to make potentially expensive decisions without adequate information or time to reflect, do not expect to succeed for very long in the markets.

I like the relationships: Traders thrive on information they glean from their network of other traders, analysts, business executives, and ordinary participants in the crowd of investors. Like hummingbirds hurrying to gather enough nectar from a great variety of flowers just to provide enough fuel for the next day of flying, traders are constantly tapping into their sources and weighing various bits of data. As they go, they must be able to separate the forest from the trees. If you do not like these kinds of interactions, do not pursue the trading life.

I like the challenge: Predicting the future is never easy. Predicting what millions of market participants will do to a specific price during a specific time period is extremely difficult. Doing it with imperfect information under real time pressure is a challenge worthy of astronauts landing on the moon. If you are not ready to try your hardest and fail as much as half the time, look for a career in a less demanding field.

How Unconscious Motives Impact Success

Don't Over Interpret Your Motives

Many people believe that psychologists place too much emphasis on unconscious conflicts that may interfere with trading performance. Surprisingly, many psychologists would agree that too much emphasis is placed on unconscious motives. It is quite possible that many traders do not have unresolved conflicts that interfere with their trading performance, or if they do, they may not be significant enough to be a problem.

A common stereotype of psychologists is that they are always trying to find a hidden unresolved unconscious conflict that underlies people's behavior. This stereotype is probably based on the misperception that the psychoanalytic theory introduced by Sigmund Freud *is* psychology. Actually, Freud had a greater influence on liberal arts and humanities than the scientific discipline of psychology. Many psychologists are critical of Freud's theories because he placed too much emphasis on unconscious processes. Nevertheless, even Freud once said, "Smoking a cigar is sometimes merely smoking a cigar." In other words, not all behavior is a reflection of an unconscious conflict.

You may not experience many unconscious processes, but everyone experiences psychological processes that occur below one's awareness. For example, while driving, people engage in several tasks that are automatic and occur below awareness. With a great deal of practice, experienced drivers can simultaneously monitor their speed, anticipate potential road hazards, listen to the radio, and talk to a friend. Similarly, in the markets, one can process several inputs in the "back of one's mind," because monitoring such inputs has been practiced over many years. Nevertheless, it is possible that decision-making and memory biases can unduly influence trading decisions, and it is vital to gain awareness of these biases to counteract them.

That said, it is important to emphasize that dynamic "unconscious processes" do, in fact, influence some people. Unconscious processes, in contrast to processes that occur below one's awareness, result from unresolved conflicts that concern extreme maladaptive needs for affiliation and self-worth. Many people, although not everyone, allow unconscious processes to guide their behavior. If these unconscious conflicts are not resolved, they will surely interfere with trading. So it's important to identify all possible unresolved conflicts and resolve them.

On the Relevance of Psychological Conflicts

How much impact can psychological conflicts have on trading? Well, sometimes they can be very influential. One of our very astute subscribers asked us, "If a trader is doing well trading, isn't it clear that he or she does not have some hidden psychological conflict? Doesn't one's trading performance speak for itself?" It's possible to achieve a high level of performance in the short term even while having psychological conflicts. One may fail in the long term, however. Consider performance in a related area: sports. Many traders say that trading is similar to playing sports. One prepares, looks for opportunities, and then reacts when appropriate. Obviously, if one is too fearful or anxious while playing sports, he or she will have difficulty performing. He or she may drop the ball or strike out, for example. So at a basic level, psychological issues have some impact. But psychological issues can also have a subtle and less obvious influence.

Consider the case of Todd Marinovich, a young quarterback for the USC Trojans in the late 1980s. His father trained him from infancy to be a star quarterback. He seemed pretty talented. For example, in the last few seconds of a close game with cross-town rival UCLA, Marinovich successfully threw a pass to a receiver and ran past the goal line while no one else seemed to spot him. The receiver then threw him the ball, and Marinovich caught it to make the winning touchdown. You've got to admit, that's talent. But what happened to him after that? He didn't seem to have his act together psychologically. He seemed to have little discipline off the playing field. He skipped classes, misused substances, and seemed to do whatever he wanted, regardless of the consequences. He sometimes argued with the coach and tried to do things his own way. USC was in the running for the National Championship that year, but lost to Notre Dame. They went on to a bowl game, but surprisingly, the coach pulled Marinovich in the middle of the game because he just couldn't maintain self-control. He wasn't in college for much longer, but folks still saw a lot of "potential" in him. After all, he was talented. The Raiders hired him as a professional player. He was there for awhile, but then he disappeared from the national spotlight. As talented as he was, he just couldn't get a handle on his own psychological conflicts. He often talked in public about how he wasn't sure who he was or of his role in society. He once said, "It's hard being Todd Marinovich."

The lesson here is that it's possible for people to be top performers in the short run, but without a true resolution of psychological conflicts, one may not continue to perform well in the long run. Perhaps this case study is an extreme example, but it makes the point: If psychological conflicts aren't resolved, they impact long term performance. Not everyone has such extreme psychological conflicts, but if you do, it's wise to resolve them. Carefully consider, "Do I know why I want to trade? Do I find trading meaningful to me? Am I clear with regard to the role I play in my family and the role I play for society?" You'll probably be a better trader in the long run if you have good answers to such questions. It's worth thinking about.

Dennis Kozlowski: A Psychological Case Study

The downfall of Tyco International CEO and Chairman Dennis Kozlowski has something to teach us about the psychology of success. Mr. Kozlowski recently resigned his position at Tyco and has been indicted on charges of conspiracy, tampering with physical evidence, falsifying business records, and sales-tax violation. Apparently, Mr. Kozlowski purchased paintings worth $13 million without paying state and local sales taxes. He took delivery of the paintings in New York, but had his art dealer ship empty boxes to Tyco's out-of-state headquarters as a decoy.

Upon reading this [initial] account, one wonders why Mr. Kozlowski would allow his career and life to be upset for such a trivial matter as the avoidance of paying sales tax. Mr. Kozlowski truly exemplifies the American dream. He came from a blue-collar neighborhood, worked his way through college, and worked his way up to head Tyco from an entry-level position. Under his leadership, he transformed Tyco from a small manufacturer of electrical conductors into one of the world's largest conglomerates. In the last four years alone, he earned $450 million in salary, options, and bonuses. His wealth afforded him a lavish lifestyle, which included helicopters as an everyday means of transportation and an exotic vintage ocean-racing yacht.

It's puzzling why Mr. Kozlowski would risk his wealth, position, and reputation to avoid paying sales tax on paintings for his art collection. This question begs for a psychological answer. Perhaps Mr. Kozlowski's behavior stems from unresolved psychological issues. Although he was successful in business, he may have felt that he did not truly deserve his success. For years, he may have felt that he could not maintain his level of success and was secretly waiting for his success to come to an end. When the end didn't come fast enough, maybe he unconsciously decided to speed things up by doing something reckless.

A different explanation is offered by the fact that the conglomerate Mr. Kozlowski worked so hard to build had not been very successful in the past year. Maybe Mr. Kozlowski's scheme to avoid sales tax was an unconscious way of quitting without admitting to himself or the business community that he really was not the "Most Aggressive CEO" as *Business Week* lauded in a cover story, or that such a leadership approach is ineffective in the current economy. Perhaps he cherished his reputation as a dominant business leader so much that he did something reckless as a way to exit Tyco, while leaving his reputation intact.

Without long-term professional psychological assessment [or knowledge of the events that unfolded since this essay was written], we can only speculate as to the true reasons for Mr. Kozlowski's behavior. However, based on our interpretation of the available information, you can see that psychological conflicts play an important role for maintaining success. One can achieve huge success, but unless one gains awareness of unresolved psychological needs and finds an adequate resolution, these unresolved issues could lead to a subsequent downfall.

The Impostor Syndrome: Feeling Unworthy of Success

In the previous section, we presented a psychological analysis of the downfall of former Tyco CEO Dennis Kozlowski. We suggested that one possible explanation for his reckless scheme to avoid paying sales tax might be a belief that he was unworthy of success, an affliction sometimes known as the impostor syndrome. Some successful people feel as if they are imposters; they have overcome personal and societal barriers to gain success, yet they feel their success was a fluke, a chance occurrence that may end at any time.

Society, close friends, or parents often give people the message that they are not worthy of success. For example, members of ethnic minority groups may have been given a societal message that they are not allowed to seek high status jobs. Women may have heard a similar message in which they were told to seek out only traditional female occupations, or people from blue-collar neighborhoods may have been told they cannot move into white-collar jobs. Although these barriers exist, they can be overcome through dedication and hard work. People with the impostor syndrome overcome these and other barriers, but they underestimate their contributions and believe that success was a matter of pure chance. Despite their success, they still believe that the societal messages they heard in their childhood are true and that they have gone to a place where they should not have gone. These prior beliefs haunt them. They tend to secretly wait for their success to come to an end.

Mr. Kozlowski, coming from a blue-collar background, may have secretly believed that he was unworthy of success. He may have felt like an impostor who was lucky to achieve a high level of success, but was also afraid that it would end. It's difficult for impostors to maintain their success because they secretly believe they do not deserve it. Because they believe success may end at any minute, they may act recklessly or take unnecessary risks, as if working under the assumption that "I might as well enjoy my success while it lasts."

It's possible that even very successful people, such as some of the presidents of the United States, may have felt like impostors to some extent and may have acted on these feelings with reckless abandon. Consider Richard Nixon who came from humble beginnings and often felt as if the higher classes of American society looked down upon him, or Bill Clinton who also came from humble beginnings and allowed several "sex scandals" to significantly upset his historical legacy.

Maintaining success is difficult if you do not believe you deserve it. Do you feel like an impostor? Do you feel that you do not belong in the occupation you have chosen? If the answer is yes, make sure you gain awareness of your feelings and find a resolution.

Protecting Your Self-Image and Reputation

We examined the downfall of former Tyco CEO Dennis Kozlowski and suggested that one reason he may have engaged in reckless behavior, such as tax evasion, was to protect his reputation. Mr. Kozlowski had a reputation as a dominant business leader who built Tyco into one of the world's largest conglomerates through a series of aggressive acquisitions. But as we have seen in the headlines, Tyco has been in a great deal of financial trouble. Some commentators have noted that Mr. Kozlowski's dominant leadership style may not have led to success after all, especially in the current economy. We suggest that Mr. Kozlowski may have unconsciously engaged in reckless behavior as a way of quitting his position at Tyco, without having to admit to himself or to the business community that the course on which he led Tyco was the wrong one.

The need to protect one's reputation is strong, and many times, people behave recklessly to protect their reputation. Many other business and political leaders have similarly behaved recklessly in an effort to protect their reputations. For example, political leaders, such as former President Clinton and Congressman Gary Condit, have tried to protect their reputations by lying about the details of their illicit affairs, and in doing so, made matters worse.

Case studies in business also illustrate people's relentless desire to protect their reputation and self-image at all costs. For example, studies show that bankers fail to write off clients' bad loans and even extend new loans, rather than admit they were wrong in their decision to advance credit to them. Leaders of major corporations have continued to put funds into failing projects because they were afraid to face the consequences of initiating projects that were unfeasible (Staw & Ross, 1987, 1989).

Reputation can influence trading decisions as well. There are numerous stories where fund managers at large institutions fail to cut their losses because by leaving the losses on paper, they can avoid admitting to themselves and others that they have made losing trades. A similar process works for the individual trader as well. An individual trader may form the identity that he or she is a "successful trader" and want to preserve this image. He or she may leave losses on paper rather than acknowledge his or her limitations.

A common stereotype is that strong business leaders face poor odds, stick to their guns, and can turn a losing proposition into a winning one. Trying to meet such an unrealistic standard, however, can lead one to continue on a losing course of action merely to save face.

Preserving one's reputation can often make matters worse and may create a viscous cycle, in which one fails to acknowledge a loss, the loss increases, and the loss becomes even more difficult to face. The need to protect one's reputation and self-image is strong, but it is important to realize this motive can have dire effects for one's success. It's important to face up to one's limitations. Facing up to them is inevitable, so one might as well do it sooner than later.

Expect Realistic Rewards

Even the most successful people seem to undermine their own success. Think of all the U.S. Presidents, politicians, CEOs, professional athletes, and famous actors who have achieved substantial success, yet blew it on a couple of preventable mistakes. There are numerous explanations for such behavior, but one possibility is expecting unrealistic rewards from one's accomplishments.

Becoming successful isn't easy. It often requires extreme self-control and discipline, along with risks and sacrifices. Humans have the ability to strive for goals through making sacrifices and delaying immediate gratification for a greater good. For example, college students and professionals may accrue a great deal of debt to gain appropriate education or credentials. Traditional work values dictate that one should postpone short-term gratification now and reap the benefits later. Many times it's worth making the sacrifices. It will pay off. But sometimes, some people may incorrectly construe the rewards for these sacrifices as more gratifying than they actually will be. When they eventually do achieve success, they may be disappointed. It's at this point that one may see very successful people undermine their own success. They may commit reckless acts in order to undo their success.

It's hard to know exactly why successful people may undermine their success through reckless acts. One reason may lie in Alfred Adler's "inferiority complex." Adler proposes that all people experience feelings of inferiority in early childhood, but some people experience greater feelings of inferiority than others. These early feelings of inferiority compel one to strive for superiority. Individuals try to cope with deep-seated feelings of inferiority through achieving superiority. Perhaps part of the dynamics around blind ambition is a secret need to satisfy feelings of inferiority.

Upward mobility and superiority over one's peers, however, requires extreme discipline and self-control. By focusing all of one's energy towards success, one may neglect important psychological needs. The person may fail to build satisfactory personal relationships or fail to develop a true and genuine sense of self-esteem. He or she may define himself or herself in shallow terms and expect his or her needs for self-respect and self-worth to be satisfied once these terms are met. This neglect may surface later in the form of undisciplined and reckless behavior. This could all have been prevented had the person developed more realistic expectations of reward. One cannot neglect his or her psychological needs now and hope that they will be satisfied later.

Humans have core psychological needs: one must appreciate oneself for who he or she is, develop the interpersonal skills to sustain long-term meaningful relationships, and understand one's true place in the society and the world. These needs can be hard to meet, but unless they are met, they will continue to haunt people. They lie in the back of one's mind, no matter how much success one achieves. So as you put in time and effort to become a successful trader, don't over-estimate the rewards your trading will bring. Even if you make a great deal of money, it won't help you satisfy your psychological needs. You have to make sure these needs are met first. There's no point in waiting. Work on satisfying these needs now.

The Origins of Self-Sabotage

In formulating his psychoanalytic theory of personality, Sigmund Freud postulated two biologically deep-rooted instincts as the driving forces behind all human behavior: life instincts and death instincts. The life instinct works on the pleasure principle. Humans are driven to seek out pleasure and avoid pain at all costs. The need for continual pleasure and gratification is a strong and pervasive motive that must be curtailed.

In *Beyond the Pleasure Principle*, Freud (1955) postulated the death instinct. The death instinct is less conspicuous and less powerful than the life instinct. Freud noted that all humans ultimately end up dead, and so it's logical to postulate, "the goal of life is death." Well, maybe. Although we may all die in the end, do people secretly strive to kill themselves? Is there a pervasive and basic human motive to seek out death and self-destruction? I doubt it. Towards the end of his life, Freud doubted it also.

Freud didn't have very much evidence to support his idea of the death instinct. All of his evidence was anecdotal. For example, he noted that his patients kept mulling over their past defeats in life rather than picking themselves up and moving forward. He also noted that many combat veterans had a difficult time forgetting past trauma experienced during battle upon returning home from war. Although this "evidence" does not necessarily support the existence of a death instinct, it does show that it is often easier for people to stay put than move forward.

It may be reassuring to know that while you are putting on your trades, there is not a core biological motive secretly compelling you to naturally destroy yourself. What are the origins of self-sabotage? The origins are socially learned rather than inherited and biological. Self-sabotage is closely related to the concept of fear of success. Individuals with a fear of success have heard societal messages that they will not succeed in certain realms. For example, women hear the message, "you can't succeed in a man's world." Ethnic minorities are told they can't break through racial barriers, and children from a working class neighborhood are told that they would be better off pursuing work in a blue-collar job. In many ways, it's much easier to stick with one's familiar environment than break out in a new direction.

It's ironic that at the heart of self-sabotage lies a strong desire to achieve success in an area that had previously been closed. Although people strive to break through a societal or psychological barrier to be more than their parents or society told them they could be, they may experience a psychological "tug-of-war" between striving for success and secretly believing the societal impositions against success heard while growing up. In the end, overcoming a fear of success concerns identifying these societal impositions, recognizing that one secretly believes them, and convincing oneself that they are false. That's a lot easier said than done, but that's part of the struggle to maintain one's existence and defeat the "motive" for self-sabotage.

How to Cultivate Your Creative Side

The Self-Actualizing Tendency

What motivates human behavior? Sigmund Freud claimed that humans are continuously motivated to satisfy basic animal needs, such as hunger, sex, and aggression. This is a very cynical view of human motivation, however. Perhaps lower animals are continuously striving to satisfy basic needs, but advances in art, literature, and science suggests that humans are motivated by a "higher-order" need: a need for self-actualization. Self-actualization is the desire for self-fulfillment, to realize all of one's potential, to become everything that one can, and to become creative in the highest possible way. Self-actualization is the highest level of psychological functioning that a human can attain. It's associated with a level of experience that is very conducive to trading. If one can develop the ability to continuously strive for self-actualization, he or she can be an astute trader.

Here is what self-actualizers are like. They are able to perceive reality more accurately, and quickly distinguish the genuine from the fake. They accept themselves, others, and nature. They lack defensiveness, phoniness, and self-defeating guilt. They are not critical of their shortcomings, but accept themselves and others for what they are; they don't try to make themselves, others, or the world conform to their expectations. They are spontaneous, simple, and natural. They extend their frame of reference beyond their own needs. They develop a mission in life, a purpose for living that doesn't deal with their own fulfillment, but with eternal problems beyond their own existence. They are autonomous, and act independently of their culture or social environment. They appreciate the basic goodness of life. They show a constant awareness of their good fortune, health, friends, and freedom. They accept what life offers and appreciate the opportunities that life has to offer.

You may see that the more self-actualized traders can be, the more successful they will become. Self-actualized traders accept themselves for what they are and the market on its terms. They look at the big picture and how they fit into it, and they appreciate their success. They enjoy the process of trading, rather than the monetary rewards, which tend to merely satisfy basic lower-order needs.

How does one achieve self-actualization? People must fulfill their basic lower-order needs before they can strive for self-actualization. Freud was right in saying that people must fulfill their basic animal needs for hunger, shelter, and safety before moving up to a higher level of functioning. It's difficult to satisfy higher order needs without first satisfying these lower-order needs. In addition to basic needs, people must also satisfy social and personal needs for love, belonging, and self-esteem. If people struggle to feel loved and struggle to find their place in society, they can never achieve self-actualization. People must also truly respect themselves for what they are. They must achieve a level of self-esteem that is genuinely based on an appreciation of their talents and skills, rather than on a desire to prove their worth to others. It isn't easy fulfilling these psychological needs, but it's essential for achieving self-actualization. If you can work to satisfy and eliminate the influence of lower order needs of hunger, shelter, love, belonging, and self-esteem, you can move up to the next level: a focus on achieving self-actualization. The best traders are those who have attained some level of self-actualization. So if you haven't achieved this level of functioning already, it's worth striving for it.

Self-Worth Isn't Net Worth

You've probably heard the saying, "Don't let your self-worth be defined by your net worth." The trouble with an old adage is that it is something one can strive for, but to quote another old saying, "It's often more easily said than done." Our self-esteem, or self-worth, is often based on our failures and successes in life. One of my favorite quotations is, "It's not the number of failures one faces that count, but how you recover." Some people have faced a few key failures in life and have never recovered, while it seems that people with high self-esteem take pride in how they have faced adversity and lived through it. People with high self-esteem seem to be insulated against failure. They've experienced a lot of it, and come out a winner, so they are no longer fazed by it. When it comes to trading, one is bound to face failure. More than anything, trading is a matter of developing a skill. Developing trading skills is hard, and one faces much more adversity than success. But it's not the failures that matter in the end, but how one recovers from failure.

Ultimately, having the ability to separate your self-worth from your performance depends on whether you have a solid and genuine sense of self-esteem. Few people have a clear and genuine sense of self-esteem and self-worth. Most people are influenced by how successful they have been recently, and feel better about themselves when others show them how appreciated they are.

Carl Rogers, an influential psychologist and a leader of the humanistic psychotherapy movement, noted that oftentimes people look outward when determining their self-worth. It usually starts in early childhood when parents place "conditions of worth" onto their children. It's as if they say, "If you do what I want, I will love you, approve of you, and only then will you have value." If conditions of worth are inflexible, people may learn that they must seek approval from others before they are allowed to believe they are valuable.

Ideally, people should receive what Rogers called "unconditional positive regard," which is similar to saying, "no matter what you do, I will accept you, and no matter what you do, you have worth." When people experience such relationships, they learn to give themselves positive regard, and feel they are valuable, according to Rogers. Unfortunately, most people continue to place conditions of worth on others. They negotiate with each other, and in some cases, say, “You give me what I want, and I’ll give you what you want.” This can translate into, “If I have money, power, or success, I can increase the odds when it comes to giving people what they want, and they, in turn, will give me approval and respect.” When such a viewpoint is taken, it’s hard not to view success as important. It’s hard not to equate self worth with net worth. From this viewpoint, one must be successful in order to have satisfactory interpersonal relationships and have a sense of self-worth. In terms of trading, it can turn into feeling, “the more money I make, the more I can be appreciated by others and feel good about myself.” This is not a very optimal way of living life. People should remind themselves that they have freedom and the right to be who they want to be, feel what they want to feel, and do what they want to do. When one truly believes that, he or she will look inward and allow his or her own values to define his or her self-worth. It may take some time, but when this state is achieved, one will no longer let one’s self-worth be defined by his or her net worth.

Finding Flow

In trading and sports, it’s known as being “in the zone.” Psychologist Mihaly Csikszentmihalyi (1997) calls peak experiences “flow.” People experience “flow” when they spend time in enjoyable activities, activities they find enjoyable for their own sake. During a flow experience, one performs above and beyond expectations. Flow is a Zen feeling. It’s similar to meditation or intense concentration. It’s an egoless state, when all your actions become automatic. You may see that if one trades in a state of flow, he or she will attain a high level of trading performance.

Dr. Csikszentmihalyi scientifically studied many samples of people who engaged in a wide variety of activities. His goal was to describe the components of flow experiences, and determine how individuals could put themselves into a state of flow. He found that some activities produced more flow experiences than others. Flow was more frequently experienced in work activities, when one is trying to solve challenging problems, and in hobbies and home activities, such as cooking, sewing, photography, or singing. Sports were also very conducive to experiencing flow. What do these activities have in common? First, they require a focused and ordered state of consciousness. One has to be completely focused on the task and not allow any distractions to break up consciousness. Rock climbers are likely to experience this type of focused attention. A rock climber must devote all attention to climbing and not be distracted by thinking of how high one is climbing or whether one will fall. Second, these activities involve an equal amount of skill and challenge. If a challenge is too great compared to one's skill, it causes worry, anxiety and a breakup of consciousness. On the other hand, if the task is too easy, it is viewed as boring.

How can trading be transformed into a flow experience? Make sure that you set up conditions to make trading fun and enjoyable. Trading certainly is a challenge, but some traders are overwhelmed, and this is not conducive to flow. The trick is finding a happy medium between trading strategies that challenge your skills, but do not exceed them. If one tries to put on big trades or use strategies and methods that are beyond one's ability, for example, flow will not be experienced. When this happens, traders feel worry and anxiety. They cannot focus complete attention on monitoring their trades.

So if you want to experience flow and perform at your highest potential, the key is to set appropriate goals. Manage your risk. Develop a well-defined trading plan based on your current understanding of the markets. Don't make trading more complex than you can understand right here and right now. Don't trade beyond your abilities. As you trade according to your current abilities and make small amounts of progress, you will experience trading as enjoyable. You will be able to focus on trading the markets with a high level of focused attention, in the same state of mind that an athlete experiences when playing sports, a dancer feels while dancing, or an artist experiences while creating art. Soon, your skills will develop even more, and you can face even more challenging trading goals. With greater and greater experience, you will find trading more enjoyable, experience greater levels of flow, and continue to hone your trading skills. Flow is an optimal state for traders. It's worth learning how you can experience more flow while trading.

Out with the Old and In with the New

"Old habits are hard to break. It's hard to teach an old dog a new trick." These sayings have a grain of truth to them. It's often difficult to abandon old ways of doing things for new ones. The successful trader, however, must be able to keep what is working and discard what isn't working. Why are old habits hard to break and how can we change them? Here are some suggestions.

Self-monitoring: It is vital that you accurately self-monitor the behaviors you want to change. It's often hard to identify behaviors that should be changed, but one cannot change a behavior unless he or she identifies precisely what that behavior is. Sometimes, however, we resist looking at our behaviors because we don't want to admit how poorly we have been doing. Some traders are afraid to carefully look at win-loss ratios, for example, because they don't want to admit they have been losing money. But we probably don't fool ourselves as well as we think we do. When things are going against us, we secretly know it. Ironically, we probably also believe that we are doing more poorly than we really are. We are probably spending more effort and psychological energy denying the truth than looking at it objectively, and taking specific action to remedy the situation. Self-examination can often be a relief, rather than a source of discomfort. We usually find that we are not doing as poorly as we had secretly envisioned, and when we look at ourselves objectively, we usually find that we can harness our resources and develop a creative solution.

Conquer neophobia: People repeat behaviors when they are rewarded, and reduce behaviors when punished. But sometimes the rewards are subtle and concern the avoidance of an unpleasant experience. Neophobia is the fear of new experiences. We associate our past experiences with safety, while anticipating new experiences with fear and doubt. Animals instinctively fear new environments as a form of self-protection, and humans sometimes fall prey to this tendency. For example, some traders believe they can only trade one market, but not another. Or they may fear that new trading strategies may be too complicated to learn. These fears may be valid, but they are probably blown out of proportion. These fears prevent traders from learning new skills, which are vital for survival in ever changing market conditions. Don't let fear of the new prevent you from learning how to trade in new markets or with new methods. Trade small positions if you need to, but get out there and try something new.

Practice alternatives: Once you have conquered your neophobia, it's time to practice new alternatives. As you practice new methods, carefully monitor how well you are doing, and have realistic expectations. If your expectations are too high, you will tend to feel as if you are failing and punish yourself for trying. By holding realistic expectations, you will naturally reward yourself when making progress, and gain mastery through experience. It's possible to learn something new if you set your mind to it. Try it, and you will see it's worth the effort.

Chapter 5

Risk Management

Trading coaches and trading books alike preach the virtues of some form of risk management, especially for novice traders. To some extent, trading is very much like gambling. There is no sure thing, so you are taking a risk every time you make a trade. What separates an amateur gambler from a professional gambler, and a novice trader from a seasoned trader, is some form of risk management plan. Novice traders and amateur gamblers are seeking out fast and easy wins. They don't really believe they will make a profit, so they are willing to risk a great deal of capital and hope they will make a killing. Professional gamblers and seasoned traders are confident that over the long term, they will have an edge, and make a profit should they place enough bets. Ideally, one should risk only a small percentage of capital on each trade. Doing so will provide some protection against a severe drawdown. The essays in this chapter are consistent with conventional wisdom in that they espouse the virtues of managing risk. But this topic is not that straightforward. Although it is beneficial for novice traders to manage risk to live through the "learning curve" of trading, seasoned traders don't always follow risk management rules rigidly. We tried to present both sides in this chapter. The challenge is to know when to risk a great deal of capital and when not to risk. These essays will help you address this challenge.

Risk Management: The Successful Trader's Secret Weapon

There are no universal rules when it comes to trading. One trader's rule is another trader's prohibition. But if there is one concept that seems to be universal across traders, it is to manage your risk. For example, Mark Boucher says, "You can have a crummy trading strategy, but if you have good [risk] management, you can make money. If you have poor risk management, it doesn't matter how good the trading strategy is, you're going to lose in the end." Christopher Tate views risk management as the key to survival: "You must have a survivability element so that if you literally wished to select stocks by throwing darts at a board, you would continue to survive market to market." The specific risk management approach differs from trader to trader, but what doesn't differ is the strong commitment traders have to money management. As Mike Quanbeck says, "If I drawdown more than 20% in the year, I'm out for the year." These quotations from the Innerworth Master Interviews suggest that risk management is the successful trader's secret weapon.

Although the specifics of risk management can differ, the basic idea across approaches is to limit the amount of money you risk on a given trade, and to determine a stop-loss point to limit your risk should the trade go against you. (Some traders suggest limiting one's risk to 1-3%, but there are no hard and fast rules, since any rule should be modified to correspond with market conditions.) By limiting risk on a single trade to a small percentage of investment capital, one can put on several losing trades before one's capital is depleted completely. Doing so helps one survive changing market conditions or trading strategies that don't pan out. It makes the probability of "blowing out your account" very low.

In addition to preserving investment capital, risk management also preserves psychological capital. When you risk only a small percentage of capital on a trade, you feel as if you can afford to lose it. As one trader put it, your risk should be so low that you tend to ask, "Why am I even bothering putting on this trade?" By limiting your risk, you literally ease the pressure you put on yourself to perform and this frees up some of your limited psychological resources. It's easier to maintain a more carefree attitude toward trading when you put less money on the line. Some novice traders may think, "Real traders would put on a large position if they thought they were right." Although it's often the case that some experienced traders put on larger positions than are reasonable based on their capital, it's not a good idea. Consider the famous trader Jesse Livermore, who often failed to manage his risk, and put on positions that risked most of his capital (Lefevre, 1993). He went through large swings of being a millionaire one day and a pauper the next. It's more important to survive to trade another day, than risk your capital on a single trade, lose it all, and be out of the game completely. So follow the advice of successful traders. Limit your risk, reduce your feelings of stress, and survive to trade on.

You Don't Always Need To Be Right

A common belief among novice traders is that one always needs to be right. Many believe that a trading strategy must always produce a profit. Although it is true that a long losing streak can wipe out one's trading account, one can actually have a large proportion of losing trades to winning trades and still be profitable. It's merely a matter of using risk management. Let's consider a specific hypothetical example to illustrate this point.

Suppose John has $150,000 to invest. He decides to arbitrarily risk 3% of his capital on each of 10 trades. He figures it is a relatively small amount that he could afford to risk and lose. He also decides to use a simple stop-loss rule: if a stock price drops below 8% of the purchase price, then sell. He then uses an arbitrary sell rule for his winning trades: If a stock increases by 20% of the purchase price, then sell. (Please note that we aren't advocating the use of these rules, we are just trying to make a point.)

Let's calculate the expected results. Approximately $4,500 is risked on each trade. If the trade loses $360, it is sold. If the trade produces a $900 profit, it is sold. If 3 out of 10 trades are winners, the overall profit (wins - losses) is (3 X $900) - (7 X $360) = $2700 - 2,520 = $180. Now, $180 isn't very much of an overall return, but you can see the point. Even by winning only 3 out of 10 trades, there is still a profit. (It's necessary, however, to use a discount broker who charges less than $5 for a round-trip trade).

This is quite a conservative strategy. One probably wouldn't want to follow it precisely. It demonstrates, however, that one doesn't always need to be right all the time to come out ahead. Nevertheless, you may see that a few modifications can make the general approach very profitable. For example, if one were to win 50% of the trades, the expected profit is (5 X $900) - (5 X $360) = $4,500 - $1,800 = $2,700. Similarly, one probably would not want to sell a winning trade merely because it reached a 20% profit. One can "let it ride a little longer" and perhaps make a 50% profit, for example. This would result in even more overall profits. The incorporation of risk management rules allows you to be wrong a lot of the time, and it is reassuring to remember this point.

So remember that you don't always have to be right to make a profit overall. Even by using a very simple set of risk management rules, and following them mechanically, you can come out ahead. The lesson is not to use such rules mechanically, but to consider how some simple planning and risk management can prevent emotions, such as anxiety and fear, from negatively impacting your trading decisions. When you are first learning to trade, risk management can help you survive, stay in the game, and allow you to hone your trading skills. As you gain more skills, you can risk a little bit more on trades you have identified as "high probability setups" and fine-tune your stop-loss or exit rules. But in the meantime, consider keeping your goals modest, with the main goal of minimizing risks, building skills, raising self-confidence, and refining your method.

Mixed Messages

Traders often hear "mixed messages" when it comes to risk management. Some traders seem to use very specific rules for managing risk, such as risking a small percentage of capital on each trade. Other traders don't seem to have any rules, and if they do, they don't seem to stick to them. They put on big positions when they believe they see a chance to make a big win. When they believe they are right, they just take a chance. It would seem that doing that could blow all your capital, if they were wrong. Novice traders are frequently confused by these mixed messages.

When it comes to trading, there is no one "right" way to trade. So if you are looking for one "true" way on how to trade, it may be difficult to find. All one can do is consider the advantages and disadvantages of each approach and decide which approach you want to take. But for a novice trader, it's often useful to listen to what most trading coaches say about risk management, which is to manage your risk.

Let's consider the advantages of risk management for a novice trader. Novice traders have not yet learned how to use a set of methods consistently to make a profit in the long term. For novice traders, it is often vital that they control their risk (for example, risking a small percentage on each trade), so that they could survive long enough to gain mastery as a trader. One reason trading coaches preach the virtues of careful risk management is that a common mistake among novice traders is wanting to "get rich quick" and putting on big trades to make big wins. The methods and skills of a novice trader, however, do not warrant taking such huge risks. What often occurs is that they lose all their capital on a few big trades and need to rebuild their capital before trading again. Rather than gaining mastery as a trader, they fruitlessly go through cycles of risking a lot, losing it all, quitting trading to rebuild capital, and so on. These novice traders never give themselves a realistic chance of learning how to trade consistently. In contrast, the novice traders who manage their risk can trade longer, and hopefully learn how to trade consistently before their capital runs out.

Once a trader becomes seasoned, he or she may want to "reach the next level" and make a lot more profit. It seems that seasoned traders reach an asymptote, at which point a self-imposed cap limits their profits. It's hard to break through this barrier, and no one really seems to know why. Very experienced traders who want to make greater profits need to start bending or breaking the rules a little to see if they can make greater profits and break through the barrier. One approach that seems to work for some traders is to identify the two to five best trading opportunities per year and bet a lot on these opportunities. This is risky, but some seasoned traders are willing to take the risk in order to make huge yearly profits. They also can afford to take more risks. As seasoned traders, they can take their remaining capital and build it back up, should they need to. They have the methods and experience to do that, but novice traders do not. The vast experience of seasoned traders also allows them to identify those rare trading opportunities that will produce a big profit, whereas a novice trader has no solid evidence for making such decisions.

Although there are no "rules" for how to trade, there are advantages for novice traders to follow some basic guidelines. One is to use some form of risk management in order to "survive the learning curve." If you are a novice trader, it is worth considering the advantages or risk management.

A Realistic Plan

Allen Brunet had it. He was tired of facing the everyday rat race: commuting in rush hour traffic 20 hours a week, struggling to balance the demands placed on him by his wife at home and his boss at work, and feeling unrewarded for his efforts. He decided, "Enough is enough. I'm going to quit my job and become a full time trader. I've got that $50,000 I inherited from my Uncle Fred, and that should be enough to get started. I can live on $20,000 a year, if I have to. How hard can that be?"

Does this story sound familiar? Many traders decided to get into this business for the freedom they could attain. They no longer had to work to satisfy their boss and meet endless job deadlines. They now could set their own hours, work when they wanted and take off when they felt like a vacation. But how realistic is this plan? Can Allen's plan work?

It may work. In *Market Wizards* (Schwager, 1989), for example, Tom Baldwin describes how he left his job as a product manager for a meatpacking firm to lease a seat on the Chicago Board of Trade. He started initially with $25,000 in 1982, and his expenses were $3,000 a month. He went on to make millions, so when you look at Allen's plan, it seems realistic. But is it really? Let's do some simple math. Suppose that Allen was able to make a 20% return on his investment, on average, for a year. Twenty percent of $50,000 is $10,000, which is half of what Allen needs to meet his basic living expenses. Indeed, based on a 20% return, Allen would need an initial stake of $100,000 to make the $20,000 he needs to meet his objectives. That assumes that he can actually achieve a 20% return, and does not face a severe drawdown. Upon closer examination, Allen's plan does not seem to be viable. He would need to trade in a highly effective manner and make a whopping 40% return on his investment to meet his objective of

$20,000 a year. Even the most seasoned traders don't make that kind of return consistently.

Even if traders make big returns consistently, it takes a psychological toll to need to perform at that level. It places too much pressure on oneself. As the character Jesse Livermore noted, when one needs to use a large percentage of capital to maintain his lifestyle, he usually fails under the strain (Lefevre, 1993). Tom Joseph's advice to new traders is, "You can't go in with the attitude that you're going to be successful overnight. Unless you're going to trade for extra income, as a hobby, don't jump in and say you're going to make trading a primary source of income so you can pay your bills. You're not going to be successful. It's too much pressure." In the final analysis, there are two things wrong with Allen's plan. He is under-capitalized for his objectives and placing too much pressure on himself to perform. So if you are new to trading, make sure that you have realistic objectives before making the transition to trading full time.

To Risk or Not to Risk

To risk or not to risk, that is the question. One has to risk money to make money. Is it better to survive losing streaks and risk small amounts of capital on each trade, or risk a lot of capital and really make a big win? There is not a single right answer to this question. (And even though we sometimes take strong positions at Innerworth, we truly believe that there is never just one right answer to any question.) Whether to risk a lot of capital or a little capital on a given trade is a personal question that you must decide based on your capital, your lifestyle, and your personality.

Consider the case of Allen Brunet who had $50,000 in his trading account. Allen was thinking about trading full time, but to do so, he had to make $20,000 a year to meet his daily living expenses. We argued that it might not be a very good idea for Allen to quit his job just yet. A return of $20,000 on a $50,000 account would be a 40% return for the year. It may be difficult to achieve such a return, considering that many professional fund managers seem to think that a 20% return is very impressive. As we said previously, it isn't impossible to make a 40% return. Indeed, we noted that Tom Baldwin started with an initial stake of $25,000 in 1982 and had personal expenses of $36,000. He obviously made quite a bit more than a 20% return on his money.

In the end, it comes down to personal preference. For Allen Brunet to make a 40% return, he would need to be willing to risk a great deal of his capital. To those traders who have low risk tolerance, risking such a large percentage might be unbearable. But for those who have a high tolerance for risk, risking a great deal of capital on a trade may seem worth it. Some traders argue that if you clearly know you are right on a trade, you should risk a lot of capital on it. That is not to say that traders should falsely believe that they are right, but rather, if after doing a substantial amount of research and preparation for a trade, if they believe it is one of the best trades of the year, they might want to risk a relatively large amount of capital on it. This is an argument worth considering. However, it is important to consider the downside. If you lose, can you afford to take the loss? If you risk such a large amount of capital, do you have the personality that can continue to objectify the trade, look at it in a calm and unemotional way, and continue to make logical decisions after the trade is executed? If the answer to these questions is "yes," that's great. But if the answer is "no," then you must adjust your trading style to suit your personality. Trading small positions, and thus, risking little on any given trade, can take a lot of the pressure off. Even if you don't have much of a tolerance for risk, if a position is small enough, it is easier to manage one's emotions and stay calm and rational while entering, holding, and exiting a trade. To each his own. But whatever you decide, think of the consequences and make sure that you can live with your decision.

Get Off the Roller Coaster

One of the ways that novice and intermediate traders evade success is to seek out risk, danger and excitement. Although it's beneficial to not be afraid to take risks, it's not a good idea to seek them out. It's quite likely that such an inclination is a warning sign that you are trading less effectively than you ought to be. Ideally, the ultimate trading system would be dull, methodical, risk-free, and even boring. The closer you get to this ideal, the easier it becomes to rack up the big gains and stay in the markets for many more years to come. Here are some suggestions to help you get off the emotional roller coaster and move into the realm of elite traders:

Try to avoid risk rather than seek it out: The central key to success in the markets is capital preservation. The longer and more successfully you can avoid major drawdowns, the better shape your account will be and the more profits you can pile up when the market moves your way. The key to avoiding drawdowns is to avoid risk.

View excitement as a warning sign: Excitement is a psychological cue that your nervous system is moving into a higher level of activity. Sometimes, you are excited because something good is about to happen. But more often than not, excitement in the markets is a warning sign that you are in over your head, trading too large, taking too much risk, or otherwise moving away from the ideal situation. Rather than enjoy your excitement while trading, seek to find out what is making you feel that way and what you can do to get rid of it.

Walk away from danger: There are plenty of things that can go wrong in the markets when you are not expecting them. Why in the world would you want to take a position that makes you vulnerable to additional things that can go wrong? Whenever you sense danger in the markets, duck and run for cover. If you are enjoying the danger, you are in the wrong business.

Remember that thrills can lead to problems in the long run: There is a special feeling in the pit of your stomach that signals you are out on the edge, being buffeted by external forces, and probably at least a little out of control. Those feelings are fun at the amusement park. In the markets, they are very often precursors to unwanted developments that will hit you in the pocketbook. Your goal should be to trade for many years without feeling any thrills at all, except the quiet thrill you experience after you completed a trade that has worked out better than expected.

Planning For Success

One important aspect of working the markets that often separates top-flight traders from the rest of the crowd is the effort they put into planning for long-term success. The most serious and active traders work very hard to develop a comprehensive plan for achieving the level of success they want. Less successful traders, in contrast, tend to trade opportunistically; they often shift from one strategy to another, making the easy trades, and trusting their instinct to guide their selection of set-ups and management of their open positions. But trading without a plan for success has many disadvantages, including that it allows a few bad decisions to unravel all the profits you have laboriously piled up over a long period of time. Instead of letting the markets drive you, consider:

Setting profit objectives: A plan for success begins with reasonable assumptions, expectations and goals. Perform the necessary calculations and establish the trading size, risk per trade, and number of trades you can afford to put on. Then keep your trading activity within the parameters you established.

Selecting trades that meet your criteria: Without a plan, nearly every reasonably good opportunity seems attractive. A plan helps you be more selective about the setups you will take, reducing wasted effort and unnecessary risk while improving the opportunities for profit in the trades you do take.

Evaluating your progress at regular intervals: Opportunistic traders can judge their effectiveness only on the basis of their account balance. Having a plan for success allows you to evaluate your trading process, behavior, and strategy, irrespective of the income you are producing at the moment.

Taking the long view: Without a plan for success, you are simply foraging for opportunities. Having a plan is more like farming, where organization and proactivity usually allow you to enjoy bigger, better, and more predictable harvests. If you want to build a stable life with long-term prospects, there are clear advantages to behaving more like a farmer.

The Value of Stops

It is a basic and powerful tool of the trading business, but it is one of the most neglected: the plain and simple stop, or stop-loss order. Actually, there are two forms of the stop: a formal stop you leave as a trading order with your broker, and an informal stop you keep in mind as prices vary, and which, depending on your own judgment, you may or may not turn into a formal trading order when the stock returns to your entry point.

There is a clear advantage to the informal stop, because savvy traders are usually able to spot the prices where large numbers of formal stop orders are accumulating. Knowing the demand built up at a certain price, they are often able to position themselves for a big gain that carries a very minimal amount of risk.

Formal stops also have their own clear advantage: they execute automatically to take you out of a position without requiring you to make a decision in the heat of market action. For many traders, this advantage outweighs the advantage of informal stops. The reason? An informal stop that you fail to execute at the right time and the right price can be dangerous to your capital. What is more, blowing your mental stop amounts to reevaluating and changing your plan, which is usually a reflection of emotion over logic and is seldom the right thing to do. To understand why, consider the reasons for using a stop: they are primarily intended to help limit your losses or to insure that you will capture at least some of the gains you already have in a position.

Markets can sometimes move so rapidly that formal stop-loss orders are hardly more effective than market orders. But in most cases, stops allow you to concentrate on other matters and feel confident you probably will not get hurt in a particular open position. While stop orders will not usually get you every penny available in a trade, they are a form of insurance that helps prevent additional and unforeseen givebacks to the market. Who is best served by stops? Traders who simply have not proven they have the ability to step out of losing positions with only small losses. Until you know you can exercise proper money management, the money management aspect of stop loss orders will help make sure you survive with enough capital to trade another day.

Exit Formulas

Every good trader has a system or methodology for determining stop losses. Such systems are usually sets of formulas and criteria by which stop loss levels are automatically set. Experienced traders go a step beyond the concept of the stop loss by using trailing stops, which are stop loss levels that are adjusted as the price changes

As part of the exit technique, the formulas and criteria used are very important to the success of a trade.

Inexperienced traders often make the wrong choices when it comes to establishing a stop loss methodology. In an effort to automate their stop loss determinations, they tend to use over-simplified formulas and/or criteria, to the point that they apply an ineffective formula believing that it'll work. In such cases, their stop loss methodology becomes a generalized, mechanical system that doesn't address its purpose. This results in miscalculated stop loss levels, which will cause the trader to exit out of a trade either too early or too late.

One of the most common and simplest methods of setting a stop loss level is to set the level as a percentage of the entry price. For example, a trader may decide that if the price reverses by 2% of his or her entry price against his or her position, he or she will exit. This type of simplified model is not very useful. If the trader is trading in high levels of volatility on a particular day, his or her stop loss levels will be completely ineffective and will cause him or her to make the wrong choices. Additionally, this type of methodology doesn't incorporate the trailing stop technique. To use a trailing stop in this example, the trader would have to adjust what he or she considers his or her entry price as the price moves in his or her favor. For example, if the price went up 2% in his or her favor, he or she would consider his or her entry price to be at the 1% mark, and therefore his or her stop loss levels would shift.

The primary purpose of your exit formula(s) is to identify the point at which your reason for entering the trade is no longer valid or at which letting your profits run beyond your profit objectives is no longer justified. And since you'll have different reasons for entering different trades, having a set of exit formulas will allow you to choose the right one depending on what reasons you entered the trade with.

Being Out Of There

One of the important differences between a serious, successful trader and someone just learning to trade the markets is the emphasis on market involvement. The "wannabe" trader feels he or she must be in the markets all the time. The successful trader has no such compulsion. He or she knows it's far safer to be out of the markets, and gets in only when the getting is good. This seems like a small distinction, but it can be huge in terms of the difference it makes in bottom line performance over the course of a year.

Just like a gambler who feels he or she must have a bet down on every sporting event, the "wannabe" trader who is always in the market is mixing the same kind of high-quality opportunities that the most expert trader will take with far lower-quality opportunities that the expert explicitly avoids. There is very little possibility that these lower-quality setups will pay off in the trader's favor.

Here are some important ways these different approaches translate into bigger or smaller account balances:

Setup standards: The beginning or intermediate trader is focused on taking the best available setups that he or she can find. That's good. But this approach inevitably includes some setups that don't offer a satisfactory risk/reward profile. The successful trader, on the other hand, takes only those setups that meet all his or her criteria. This rules out losses from lower-quality opportunities. The almost automatic result is better trading choices, and higher earnings.

Less exposure: The beginning or intermediate trader is willing to accept all manner or risks, most especially those that aren't quite apparent or quantifiable. In other words, he or she is trading when the market is predictable, and he or she is also trading when the market is not so predictable. There's no way that his or her results can equal that of the experienced, successful trader who specifically avoids uncertain, unpredictable market situations. Because the successful trader is out of the markets unless he or she can quantify the risk, he or she accepts far less risk, overall. This puts a much smaller cap on losses from the trades that don't work out as expected. The almost automatic result is smaller drawdowns, fewer givebacks to the market, and larger account balances - even without any extra winners.

Stop Dependence

As a trader, you always hear about how important it is to incorporate stop loss methods into your trading plan. It has been shown time and time again that using trailing stops are critical to your success. But at the same time, as with any other tool, if used improperly, stops can cause traders to take far more losses than they might otherwise take. Many traders have or develop dependence on their stop loss methods, such that they use them as a security blanket for the decisions they make. This causes them to be less diligent with their decisions because they get the sense that they have a safety net.

If you're stop dependent, you'll feel more confident about the decisions you make, because you'll figure that you're not going to lose much simply because you have a stop loss methodology and know that you'll stick to it. With this additional confidence, you'll be quicker to make decisions and will not properly conduct your analyses and evaluations. This is equivalent to unjustifiably taking on more risk. And because traders who become stop dependent are not very experienced risk managers, they'll easily fall into a trap of seeking risk beyond their means.

Because you feel more confident about the decisions you're making (and therefore find them easier to make) and your risk threshold is low, you'll inevitably end up making more trades than you might otherwise make. The majority of these trade decisions will not be profitable ones because your analysis of the trade scenario was flawed from the start. But at the same time, you limit your losses by stopping out. In the mid to long term, you'll find yourself taking a lot of smaller losses, one after another, such that you end up losing a whole lot more than if you didn't feel like you had the security or safety net of your stop loss methodology.

It's important to understand that the purpose of setting trailing stops is to control risk and limit the results of a bad decision. Stopping out is still the same as taking a loss; it does not correct an incorrect decision in any way. And it's even more important to understand that using a good stop loss methodology is critical to your trading success. The key is to use your stop losses in the capacity they're intended for and not as a safety net for your decisions.

Roomy Trading Plans

Successful traders tend to have a specific routine when it comes to their trading plan. Whether they're making a long-term trade or looking for intraday opportunities, their methodology in evaluating trades or investments doesn't leave much room for making last minute decisions; it's more of a process of following a series of rules.

Novice traders often have difficulty developing such systematic trading plans. They tend to come up with routines or plans that leave a lot of room for last minute decision-making, and which usually cause them to fall into common psychological traps and make incorrect decisions. This is because they don't understand how to set rules for what they view to be innumerable unknown factors that they think will only become apparent as they watch a specific price pattern.

They figure that they need to and can "fill-in" their trading plan at the last-minute, such that each decision is made partly based on a "plan" and partly based on other decisions and assessments made right before entering the trade. Successful traders on the other hand, have learned that if they need to "fill-in" the details of their plan at the last minute, their plan is structured incorrectly.

Last-minute observations and considerations can easily cause the trader to fall into common psychological traps. Since the trader tries to quickly factor these into his or her incomplete trading plan, potential emotional influences (like fear, greed, hope, and panic) become a real part of his or her decision-making. In addition, the trader is more susceptible to media influences and will have difficulty properly assessing and sticking to risk ratios and stop-loss points. Therefore, what seems to the trader to be a planned, objective decision is really an emotional one. Many times, the losses resulting from such decisions will cause the trader to lose any confidence he or she may have had and to believe that he or she doesn't have what it takes to become a successful trader. This can lead to other longer-term psychological issues.

The key to prevent this from happening to you is to very critically evaluate what you believe to be a good trading plan. How much of the decision-making is done immediately before your trade? What kind of observations and assessments does your plan require you to make, and how susceptible are they to emotional and outside influences? Answering these types of questions will help you properly evaluate the effectiveness of your trading plan.

Chapter 6

Controlling Your Emotions

The stereotype of an ideal trader is a cold, rational decision-making machine, a person who doesn't allow emotions and passion to guide trading decisions. This robotic ideal is often hard to achieve. After all, traders are humans, and humans are guided by their emotions. Scientists who study emotions are quick to point out that emotions play an important role in the decision-making process. Many times, humans must make quick decisions to survive. When you see a mugger on the subway, for example, your instincts serve you well if they activate your central nervous system, and help you get out of there quickly. When it comes to trading, however, emotions may be a little more of a hindrance. Emotions are something you must strive to control, but it isn't easy. It's natural to feel fear when you see a trade turning against you, pride and elation when you make a big win, or sadness and disappointment when you have a severe drawdown. In this chapter, we present a variety of essays on emotion. Some focus on how fear, hope, and greed drive market prices in terms of mass psychology, while others focus on how an individual can identify and control his or her specific emotions, such as anger, frustration, envy, and disappointment. All traders have issues regarding emotion control to some extent, so it's important to determine where you stand and develop an emotion control plan that fits your needs.

Change Your Viewpoint, Change Your Emotions

Trading coaches suggest a variety of ways to control emotions. These approaches tend to focus on simply gaining awareness of emotional processes, and through this awareness, it is assumed that emotions can then be controlled. Although these approaches may work for weak transient emotional states that dissipate quite easily, they are less effective for more enduring and intense emotional states. These states require a more complex approach, such as a cognitive-behavioral therapeutic approach. Applying this more sophisticated framework will help you manage a variety of emotions for the long term.

The prominent psychologist Albert Ellis (1962) claims that emotions are the result of how we interpret events, rather than the objective events themselves. Consider the following example. Suppose you went to the bank to cash a check and after waiting in a long line for almost an hour, the bank teller said there was no cash left in the bank. Most people would be a little upset and perhaps angry. They have an expectation that a bank should always have money. After all, isn't dispensing cash one of the main functions of a bank?

Let's use this situation to understand what Dr. Ellis means when he says that it's the way people think about events that makes them angry, rather than the events themselves. Dr. Ellis would argue that it is not the event itself, the bank running out of money, but your belief that "the bank should always have money" that makes you upset.

If you were to refute or challenge this belief, you would not feel upset. For example, you may think, "Perhaps the bank should always have money, but people make mistakes. Someone made a mistake and I should expect mistakes. It may be unfortunate that the bank ran out of money, but it isn't terrible or a catastrophe. I can find another way of getting cash."

Can you see that by changing your viewpoint, you can change your emotions? Dr. Ellis argues that there are core sets of irrational or maladaptive beliefs that make people feel upset, disappointed, or angry. By questioning and refuting these beliefs, people can change unpleasant emotions into pleasant ones, or prevent an emotionally arousing event from producing an emotional response.

Many of the negative emotions experienced during trading can be traced to specific sets of beliefs. It is worth reviewing some key beliefs. The first one, "I should be thoroughly competent, adequate, and achieving in all possible respects," is a maladaptive belief that can cause unpleasant emotions. People who hold this belief may tend to think that they should never make a trading mistake, that they should be able to anticipate every possible flaw in their trading strategy, and that they should be successful in anything they set out to do. To some extent, these beliefs are adaptive. If we didn't hold these beliefs to some extent, we would not be very successful.

However, when these beliefs are taken to an extreme, we are bound to feel upset, and many times it is unnecessary. It is important to identify when beliefs and expectations are too extreme. For example, a person does not need to be *thoroughly* competent, adequate, and achieving in *all possible* respects. This is a standard that no one can meet. It is useful to be as competent as possible, but competent in "all possible respects" is impossible. This kind of thinking will surely make you feel upset when you do not live up to your expectations. When you fail to live up to your expectations, it is adaptive to allow yourself to make some mistakes and forgive yourself for doing so.

Other maladaptive beliefs that are pertinent to trading are, "If things do not go or stay the way I very much want them to be, it would be awful, catastrophic, or terrible." Holding this belief will make you feel guilt or disappointment when you lose money on a series of trades. When things do not go your way, it may be slightly unpleasant, but it is not a catastrophe. A more adaptive belief is, "Things didn't go my way, but I'm going to focus all my energy on making things turn out fine."

Another popular maladaptive belief is, "Unhappiness is externally caused and I cannot be happy unless I control events." On the contrary, unhappiness is *internally* caused, and once we acknowledge that our thinking is the actual cause of our feelings, we can change our feelings, despite the many unhappy events we may encounter.

Similarly, people tend to believe, "One should remain upset or worried if faced with a dangerous or fearsome reality." This belief results in traders feeling upset for long periods after a series of losing trades. However, it is not necessary to remain upset and worried when facing a series of losing trades. Such emotions are reasonable, but are not productive. Once you understand that it is not necessary to remain upset, and that by changing your thinking, you can change your emotions, you will be able to control your unpleasant emotions, even when the equity in your account is down.

Consider refuting other beliefs, such as, "It is easier to avoid responsibilities and difficulties than to face them" and "There is invariably one right, precise, and perfect solution and it would be terrible or catastrophic if this perfect solution were not found."

When you are feeling unpleasant emotions, such as disappointment, despair, or guilt, it is probably one of these core beliefs that lie behind it. Identify it, refute it, and change your emotions.

An Objective and Analytic Approach

Trading the markets takes a lot of nerve. Decisions often need to be made quickly, and if one flinches, one may miss a significant price move, and divert a sound trading plan. Fear and anxiety often are at the root of hesitation. One may fear a loss, fear being wrong, or fear not having an opportunity to exit. The more a trader can control fear and anxiety, the more he or she can avoid the tendency to hesitate. A classic experiment on the study of emotion control provides a solution. One of the best ways to control fear and anxiety is to take an objective and analytic approach to interpreting events.

In the 1960s, Professor Richard Lazarus (1964) and colleagues elicited fear in a laboratory setting by showing participants films portraying various stressful situations. They called one of these films the "sub-incision film." In this film, an Australian Stone Age tribe demonstrated a primitive ritual in which crude surgical operations were performed on young men as a rite of passage. Participants watching the film knew these crude incisions were going to be made, but they didn't know exactly when. Physiological measures of fear, such as skin conductance, respiratory functions, and heart rate, were monitored as participants watched the film. As might be expected, levels of fear were highest at the point when the incision was made. But fear was also very high while anticipating the fearful event. Anticipation of a stressful event is often associated with fear and anxiety. After the incision, fear immediately decreased. The vantage point from which participants viewed the film exerted a powerful influence on emotional experience. By manipulating the soundtrack of the film, and coaching participants on how to cope with watching the incisions, researchers were able to help people manage their emotional reactions. One approach was to "intellectualize" the film. Participants tried to view the film as a scientific documentary in which one removes oneself from the ongoing process and tries to look at the events from a rational and impersonal perspective. A second approach was to try to "think positively." Subjects were told to focus on the positive aspects of the film. For example, the young men in the ritual looked forward to it, and were viewed as having a higher status in the tribe once the ritual was completed. Results showed that taking an objective and intellectual approach was much more effective at controlling emotions than trying to think positively and trying to ignore the negative aspects of the film.

This research study shows how taking an objective approach to trading can reduce fear, and in turn, reduce hesitation. Any way that you can objectify or intellectualize trades will improve your ability to control fear. For example, looking at trades as a percentage of increase or decrease in capital rather than dollar amounts can help greatly. Don't think of the value of the money and what it can purchase. Look at it as merely objective percentage points of loss or gain. This will help you remain rational and calm. It will help you control your fear, and reduce your tendency to hesitate.

Avoid Seeking Revenge

Getting Even With the Markets

Trading decisions are frequently influenced by fear, hope, greed, and regret. But sometimes decisions are motivated by anger. After a losing trade, you've probably heard people say, "I'm going to get even with the markets." Perhaps, you have said this yourself. The need to get even and seek revenge is a reflection of anger. People experience anger when they feel that they have been unfairly wronged (Lazarus, 1991). Traders become angry at the markets because they believe that the markets, and the people involved in the markets, should make their investment profitable. When the profits don't materialize, they implicitly or explicitly believe that the markets have wronged them.

Anger can be a dangerous emotion. When people are angry, they are ready to put up a fight. They focus all their energies on fighting, seeking revenge, and looking for any sign of provocation. It's hard to think clearly when one is angry. Sound decision-making requires the avoidance of such emotions.

There's no reason to be angry at the markets. It's important to recognize the reasons for our anger. By doing so, we will feel less anger in the long run. Here's how you can be less angry at the markets.

Don't personify the markets: Anger is an interpersonal emotion. We are usually angry with someone because we believe that he or she has purposely tried to harm us. The markets may consist of people making trades, but it doesn't make sense to treat the markets as an interpersonal setting. The people participating in the markets may engage in actions that thwart your goals, but their actions are not directed toward you personally. It is best to look at the markets as an abstract impersonal entity, rather than a collection of people.

Eliminate preconceptions: Anger is felt when our expectations have been shattered. One expects to profit from a trade, and when the profits are not realized, he or she may become angry, seek revenge, and want to get even. However, it isn't useful to have high expectations in the markets. Don't depend on the markets to fulfill your goals or meet your expectations. Assume that anything can happen. Indeed, in dealing with the markets, it's almost a given that you will lose money, so it is not useful to expect to make money on every trade. Just accept what you can get. Eliminate any preconceptions you have regarding the outcome of a trade.

Accept losses: People have great difficulty accepting a loss. The old adage, "Cut your losses short and let your profits run" reflects traders' inability to accept a loss. However, if you cannot accept a loss, you will feel anger and want to get even. Expect to lose and be ready to accept losses.

Following these guidelines will help you manage your anger. If you can manage your anger, you will feel less stress, make more rational decisions, and enjoy trading.

Don't Fight the Market, Flow with It

As traders, we often see ads and hear comments that imply that trading requires an oppositional or antagonistic stance toward the markets. Trading under the assumption that you're "fighting" the market will lead to poor decision-making and a heightened probability of panic. Fighting is generally an activity that increases your adrenaline, taps into your emergency instinctual response, and is a source of stress. Successful, experienced traders know that this disposition is damaging to their trading capacity.

You need to "work with the market" to succeed. Whether you're trading equities, futures, options, or commodities, it's critical that you "feel the market" just like you would feel your own emotions. Feeling the market means intuitively understanding price movement and patterns, such that you can literally "sense" what follows given a specific situation. Supported by your technical knowledge, this intuitive understanding will lead you to make winning decisions.

Consistently achieving this mental state requires a calm, meditative approach that coordinates your technical and creative abilities with the changing market situation. One of the key techniques to achieving this mental state is to focus on the market as a whole, rather than on any of its specific parts. You're already studying the micro aspects of patterns when you're applying technical signals, developing stop loss points, risk/reward ratios, etc. Those all come with your trading plan. The key is to identify with the overview of the market. When looking at charts or price data, the ebbs and flows of your thought patterns should correspond to those of the market, so that you can accurately apply your trading plan. Successful traders have mastered this approach.

It's important to note that there are potential pitfalls in developing and taking on this mentality. Many traders often find that their ability to achieve a meditative state of mind is sometimes negatively influenced by factors in their personal lives. While trading, you need to remove these potentially influential elements from your psyche and take on a 100% focused flow mentality.

As with most other trading and investing skills, achieving the ability to experience a focused flow requires persistence, commitment, and a lot of practice. Although it can be naturally developed over years of experience, it can also be developed through the active study of historical data. Closely evaluate the thoughts behind the trades you make and accordingly adjust your approach to achieve peak performance.

Emotional Guidebook

Emotions can get in the way of sound decision-making. The two most prevalent emotions are fear and greed, but other emotions, such as disappointment, frustration, and anger also adversely influence sound investment decisions. It's useful to be aware of the emotions one experiences and learn to control them. But it's also useful to consider how emotions can be used to enhance your trading performance.

Although a widely held belief is that emotions and rationality don't mix, this need not be the case. Emotions may have helped primitive humans and wild animals adapt, but they also play an important role in everyday life. From a social-evolutionary standpoint, emotions are efficient ways of processing interpersonal and social interactions. Each emotion arises within a particular interpersonal encounter (Lazarus, 1991). We experience fear when we perceive a threat to our well being, greed when we see an opportunity to raise our sense of well being, and disappointment when we perceive a loss to our well being. We may feel frustration when we perceive an obstacle prevents us from achieving a goal, and anger when we perceive that obstacle was unnecessary and placed intentionally in our path by another person. We feel guilt when we perceive that we have committed an act that is inconsistent with our values, and pride when we achieve a goal of personal significance.

Emotions are important and significant motivators of behavior. Without emotions, we are not alive. But emotions seem to get a "bad rap" in the trading literature. An ideal trader is a person who acts with calm and complete rationality. He or she is in complete control, disciplined, and unemotional. Striving to reach this ideal may be beneficial, but is it realistic? In the field of psychiatry, such a person is described as having obsessive-compulsive personality disorder. The person with this psychiatric disorder lives an existence similar to the fictional character of the Vulcan, "Mr. Spock." The person searches for rules, consistency, and irrefutable if-then relationships between inputs and outputs. Some say these individuals make suburb engineers or bookkeepers; in these professions, there are clear-cut rules that must be applied without exception. But this isn't true in the markets, and obsessive-compulsive people don't thrive in such situations. Besides, there is a reason obsessive compulsiveness is labeled as a psychiatric disorder: it's not very adaptive. In the end, you must learn to "use" your emotions as a guide, rather than strive to eliminate them. Recognize that each emotion arises from the "unconscious" perception you have of reality. Emotions can be an efficient way of processing information if you learn to "listen" to them. If you can develop this skill, emotions can be a useful signal, rather than something to avoid or eliminate.

Professionalism Means Less Emotion

It is the amateurs who experience and express most of the passion concerning what they do. Hobbyists will talk endlessly about their model trains or their ham radios. Backyard mechanics will discourse about their engine swaps and antique car restorations. Part-timers will obsess about the next time they can go skiing or SCUBA diving. People new to golf or other sports will experience a series of emotional ups and downs as they perform better, then worse, and better again. But professionals are different: they try to take emotions out of the picture. And this is often a good thing. Let's face it, you don't want your surgeon worrying about whether or not he or she will botch your upcoming appendectomy, then giving his or her assistants a high-five after a successful operation. Instead, you want them cool, calm, and totally in command of themselves. Serious, active traders cultivate the same kind of cool, dispassionate attitude toward their trading decisions, and the results those decisions produce. Here is a list of things serious traders do to produce and maintain this cool and dispassionate attitude.

Gains: Making money as a trader is a great feeling. But for serious traders, who have made money quite a few times before, the glory and adrenaline rush tends to fade to a general level of satisfaction. The plain fact is that making money is the object of your trading activities, so there is no way you want it to become a big emotional issue.

Losses: As with gains, serious traders will not waste a lot of emotional energy regretting losses or punishing themselves for taking them. No trader is right 100% of the time, so losses are an inevitable part of the business. To stay the course, serious traders try to focus on their activities, strategies, and immediate opportunities, rather than dwell on past losses and allow their emotions to drain away their energies.

Tough decisions: Successful traders very often owe their extraordinary incomes to some very difficult decisions they have made correctly, and at the right time. That is one of the reasons professional, active traders cultivate their decision-making skills and try to separate their emotions from the process. Too much fear, hesitation, concern, or caution usually has the effect of hampering, rather than enhancing your ability to make the tough decisions that generate the biggest rewards.

Difficult markets: Anybody can get rich (for a while) in a 9-year bull market. It's far more challenging to make money from trading in a choppy or unpredictable market environment. Serious, active traders understand the importance of persevering through any episodes of frustration, fear, or unrealistic expectations.

Controlling Fear and Anxiety

Cracking under Pressure

Whether it is trading or playing sports, when the pressure is on, many of us crack under the strain. Consider the Olympic performances of Sarah Hughes and Michelle Kwan in the 2002 Winter Olympics. Michelle tried to meet high expectations of winning the Gold Medal and made several mistakes in her performance. Sarah, on the other hand, went into her performance with fewer expectations and a carefree attitude. She said, "I really thought there was no way in the world I would win. Realistically, there was this little window, but I didn't think I would win. I went out and just skated." By taking this carefree attitude, she skated freely and without worry. This stance allowed her to react to the moment, express her creativity, and win the Gold Medal. It's like saying, "I didn't worry about how much money I would make, I just traded." It's also similar to something Andy Bushak said in his Innerworth Master Interview about successful traders on the floor of the Chicago Mercantile Exchange: "They don't have too many rules for themselves. They keep it simple, do a little bit of homework, and simply react to market conditions." In other words, they just trade.

Successful traders make trades in a carefree manner. They don't put pressure on themselves to succeed. They don't believe they need to be right, and they don't need to predict the future behavior of the market. Instead, they objectively observe market conditions, react to them, and let the market take them where it wants them to go. Successful traders are "in the zone" as Mark Douglas claims. In his book, *Trading in the Zone*, Douglas (2000) notes that seasoned traders do not doubt or second-guess themselves. They freely enter and exit trades without worrying about the consequences. This carefree approach to trading allows them to see trading opportunities more easily and allows them to take advantage of these opportunities when they arise.

How does one enter the zone? It takes intense concentration and focus, and it's difficult to maintain this stance when the pressure is on you to perform. Mark Douglas suggests removing some of the pressure by thinking in terms of probabilities and carefully managing risk. You may not win on any single trade, but after a series of trades, you will have enough wins to make a profit in the long run. Remembering this and having confidence that your trading strategies, or edges, will ensure you make money in the long run and help you stay in the zone. It's also important to manage your risk. Specifically, determine your risk on a given trade before making it, and risk only a small amount of trading capital on a single trade. Doing so will take some of the pressure off, allowing you to be more open to see the opportunities that the market offers. Be open-minded. Remember that the market is always right. It's your job as a trader to see what the market is doing, rather than imposing your will or expectations on to it. Flow with the market. Move with the market. React to the market. Let the market tell you where it wants you to go. By easing some of the pressure, you will feel more free and open. You will be able to identify trading opportunities, quickly react, and take home the profits.

Fear and Hope: Two Emotional Tendencies Driving Market Decisions

A basic premise of technical analysis is that fear and greed drive market prices. These emotions influence trading decisions regarding whether to buy or sell. When investors fear prices will decrease, they sell. When they fear an opportunity to make a profit may be missed, they buy without good reason, according to Martin Pring (1993). Greed, in contrast, arises from a combination of overconfidence and a desire to achieve profitable results in the shortest possible time frame. When traders perceive they can make a quick and easy profit, they buy.

Dr. Hersh Shefrin (2000), a prominent behavioral economist, argues that fear and greed do not drive financial markets entirely. Fear does indeed play a role, but traders react less to greed and more to hope. When traders are fearful, they focus on unfavorable aspects of a trade. For example, during a losing trade, one thinks, "I wonder how much further the price can go against me. Can things get any worse?" Hope is the polar opposite of fear. When traders feel hope, they focus on favorable aspects of a trade. They think, "I wonder how much money I'm going to make on this trade?" They count on making money, rather than continually worrying about how much money they are going to lose.

People trade to fulfill personal or financial goals, according to Dr. Shefrin. When traders decide to make an investment, they hope it will help them achieve their goals. If the investment is successful, hope turns into pride. However, if an investment is unsuccessful, hope turns into fear, and fear turns into regret. The tendency to experience hope when evaluating investment alternatives is quite different from the tendency to experience fear, but both tendencies exist in everyone. Dr. Lola Lopes (cited in Shefrin, 2000), however, suggests that one tendency predominates over the other. There are individual differences; some people tend to be optimistic and hopeful while others are pessimistic and fearful.

Dr. Lopes believes that a need for security may underlie these differences. Some people do not view their surroundings as stable and secure. They believe that their environment can change at any minute, so they are on the look out for any sign that may indicate change, which in turn could lead to instability and possibly chaos. These individuals believe they cannot tolerate an unstable environment, so they avoid it at all costs. This leads them to be on the look out for a loss. They constantly fear that they may lose money. In contrast, individuals who believe that their environment is safe and stable aren't very concerned about potential changes or possible instability. They believe they can cope with any possible change. This allows them the freedom to focus solely on the profit potential of an investment. They are optimistic and believe they are going to make a great deal of money. It's optimal to be in the middle of these two extremes. Nevertheless, emotions clearly influence trading decisions. Remember, however, it is not merely fear and greed, but hope as well.

Fighting Fear

Fear rears its head in many different ways. Fear can make you hesitate to pull the trigger on a potentially successful trade. It can make you hold onto a position when your rational mind is screaming for you to get out. Fear can sap your confidence, make you question the validity of your trading method, and even drive you entirely out of trading. Many people mistakenly feel that some people are fearful, while others aren't. The truth, as most certifiable heroes suggest, is that some people let fear dictate their actions, while others, still feeling the fear, simply do not give in. For most traders, fear is a constant companion. And that's understandable, because you are risking serious amounts of money on relatively uncertain events where with only a small mistake or a brief moment of inattention, you can give back all you have earned in the markets and more. So the trick is not to try and ignore your fear. Instead, it is better to accept your fear, within limits, and find ways to fight against it and work around it. Here is a list of ways to work around fear.

Keep fear out of your decision-making: Successful trading requires extremely accurate decision-making, a skill that is greatly compromised when fear is in the driver's seat. Most successful traders have learned to identify when they are afraid, and what they fear. Then they can introspect to make sure their fear is not the major component of their urge to take or pass on a certain choice.

Channel your fear and let it motivate you: Fear is one of the most basic animal drives to which we are subject. You are not going to be able to root it out, but you can convert that animal urge for safety into extra motivation to recheck your calculations, rethink your trading plan, and reevaluate your alternative courses of action. The net result will be better trading, as well as a greater sense of security.

Transform your fear into sensitivity: As fear builds up, your awareness is focused on sources of threat and nothing else. In practical terms, this means you are far more aware of a variety of sensory inputs than when you are feeling comfortable and safe. In a more calm, comfortable, and safe feeling state, you can dive deeper into the mass psychology behind the chart patterns you are observing, and take more accurate readings from what other traders are saying and doing. The more alert you can be when you trade, the more likely you are to observe a profitable opportunity that would otherwise escape you. Above all else, find a way of developing an awareness of your fear. You can't fight fear unless you know it is attacking you.

How to Deal With Fear

It is said that both cowards and heroes experience great fear. The difference is that one lets fear dictate their subsequent actions, while the other does not. This is important to understand because trading is definitely a fear-inducing activity. Most of us find it very easy to study, practice and paper-trade with a high degree of confidence, but when we put real money at risk, a great wave of fear engulfs us, and threatens our ability to trade effectively. So how do successful traders (and other heroes) deal with their fear? Consider some of these techniques:

Identify the source: Most traders are afraid, simply and understandably, of losing money. But once you get beyond that obvious formulation, you realize there are much more complex situations and outcomes that raise the hackles on your neck. Some of these include lifestyle compromises, blowing out your account and not being able to raise the money to get back in, looking foolish in front of your family, colleagues, and friends, or getting outsmarted by other traders. The more accurately you identify exactly what you are afraid of, the more likely it is that you can find an effective way to deal with the fear.

Consider the worst possible consequences: Once you have identified what you are afraid of, begin to visualize the details of the worst possible consequences that could result. The more vividly and precisely you conjure up what might happen to you if your fear becomes reality, the better. It is all fodder for finding a perfect fix.

Contrive remedies and safeguards: Work directly from the list of negative outcomes you do not want to face. For each one, think of ways to eliminate the negative aspects of it, circumvent it, or counter it. For example, for the fear of losing all your money, one remedy might be to reserve some and keep it away from all risk. If you think long and hard enough, every fearful possibility can yield to some kind of hopeful palliative or remedy.

Don't think, act: With your plans and safeguards in place, do not let your fear dictate your actions. If necessary, trade smaller than normal sizes. Try to develop automatic reflexes that help you follow your trading plan in even the most stressful situations. As you gain confidence and psychological strength, you will find you can trade larger and larger positions without striking up the fear that once threatened your trading effectiveness.

How to Conquer Fear

It's sometimes difficult to control fear when you have a great deal of money on the line. That's why most traders tend to risk small amounts of capital on any single trade. Putting less money on the line with each trade is an effective way to decrease the fear of losing money. But controlling fear may not be that easy for everyone.

Fear can be an adaptive emotion. We are fearful when we perceive that some harm will come to us. The experience of fear quickly and efficiently informs us that we are about to face impending doom. Some people, however, are fearful too often and too intensely. For these people, fear is something they must strive to control.

Dr. Ari Kiev (1998) offers a quick and sometimes effective way of controlling fear in *Trading to Win*: Acknowledge you are afraid and the feeling will pass. Refusal to acknowledge fear allows the feeling to perpetuate. Admitting that you are afraid will allow the feeling to dissipate.

For some people, this simple advice will work well, but for others, a more complex and systematic approach must be taken. The tendency to experience fear has a biological and genetic basis. Fear is related to the fight-or-flee response. It's a very basic response that animals use to survive in the wild and it's controlled by very primitive parts of the brain. You can see that in a crucial sense, the fight-or-flee response can be very adaptive. When harm is perceived, a wild animal must mobilize resources and make a quick decision to either fight the opponent or flee to safety.

Humans differ in their ability to control the fight-or-flee response. Some people are easily excited. Their nervous systems are rapidly aroused and once energized, calming down is difficult. Other people tend to remain calm across a wide range of situations, even those that would frighten most people. It takes a lot to get their nervous system aroused and energized.

For example, suppose you have difficulty forgetting some of your early trades where you had lost a great deal of money and that you sometimes remember these trades and become fearful. This is a common symptom among people who have difficulty controlling their fear. A series of past events coincided with fear, so that now, when people face a similar event, they continue to experience fear. An event that was once "neutral" and non-anxiety provoking now elicits fear. In this case, the fear response is "associated" or "classically conditioned" to the trading environment. When one enters a trade, one automatically and instantly becomes fearful. The feeling may be overwhelming and seem impossible to control.

An effective procedure psychologists have used to combat excessive fear is called "systematic desensitization" or "counter-conditioning." In essence, this procedure capitalizes on the fact that it is impossible to experience both the fear response and the relaxation response simultaneously. By preventing the fear response from occurring by feeling relaxed, a previously fearful event will lose its potency and no longer elicit fear.

Here's how this approach can be used. Many people with this affliction often experience fear when they put on a trade. That's the fear response kicking in. If they continue to execute real trades, they will probably continue to experience fear. Instead, they can try putting on a trade where there is no risk: trade on "paper." One pretends he or she is putting on a trade, but does not put any money at risk, and thus, feels little fear. At this point, one can practice relaxation. A relaxation procedure can be as easy as taking a few deep breaths or tensing and releasing your muscles. The key is to experience relaxation instead of fear.

Once one is able to control his or her fear while trading on paper, he or she is ready to up the ante. He or she can now put on a small trade with minimal risk. One should try to relax in order to prevent the fear response from occurring. If one becomes fearful, he or she should go back to trading on paper until, once again, he or she can prevent the fear response from occurring by using a relaxation procedure. One should gradually execute trades that require greater risk and work one's way up until he or she can put on a relatively risky trade without experiencing fear. Think of trades as rungs on a ladder that vary from little or no risk to greater and greater risk. If you experience fear at a higher rung, don't move up the ladder, move down a rung. Only after one has mastered that level, should one try to move up to a higher risk trade. By using this systematic approach, one will be able to learn to control fear and prevent fear from interfering with decision-making.

An Avalanche of Anxiety

Trading is serious business. And doing it successfully, well enough to earn a good living, can lead you into situations that have the potential to produce a significant amount of anxiety.

With the pressure and the high stakes involved, even the most well adjusted trader can sometimes succumb to anxiety attacks. But that kind of anxiety can interfere with following your plan, greatly diminish your emotion control, and seriously disrupt your trading.

To prevent anxiety build-up, follow these simple guidelines:

Relax when trading: The human animal has not evolved for trading. The pressure, the fast pace, the chaotic environment, and the heavy influence of factors beyond our control all combine to tense our muscles, fatigue our brains, and wrench our emotions. Unless you learn to avoid these outcomes, you'll end the trading day a wreck, and you'll burn out well before your time. The best approach is to develop your relaxation techniques, and to practice them regularly before, during, and after the trading day.

Focus on real facts and likely scenarios: Anxiety builds strength most often in a world of its own, where the threat of being hit by lightning seems as real and immediate as being hit by a car in heavy traffic. One of the best antidotes to anxiety, therefore, is a strong dose of reality: real facts, real analyses, and real appraisals of what's likely to happen. As a trader, you make money only when you anticipate what the real world is going to do. Capitalize on this natural ability by paying close attention to reality factors, and letting the fantasies sent forth by your anxieties wither on the vine.

Stay in the moment: One source of anxiety is the possibility that your trading luck will abandon you, that your ability to make money will dry up, and that your track record as a successful trader will not carry forward into the future. Since you can never know whether or not this anxiety will actually play out, it's counter-productive to waste too much time thinking about it. Instead, stay focused on day to day issues: what setups to take, where to exit, and how to control your risk. If you manage your short-term success well enough, your long-term success will take care of itself.

When anxiety arises, go back to basics: It's possible that your anxiety is not entirely off base, and your instincts or subliminal perceptions are correctly telling you that something is amiss. If you feel this might be the case, consider temporarily stepping back from your trading to deal with the issue. You may want to exercise, or occupy yourself with something routine while your mind runs free to explore where the anxiety is coming from, and what it will take to resolve it.

Jealousy and Envy

Keeping Up With the Joneses

Do you ever compare yourself to your friends and colleagues? It's quite common to compare ourselves to others so as to see if we measure up. We may feel envious when a friend or neighbor seems to be doing better or jealous when others have gotten more of the limited resources that we are also after. What happens when you find out a friend or colleague is making more money in the markets than you are? Do you feel jealousy, or envy? Do you wish you had made as much money in the markets? In trading, it's natural to want to compare ourselves to others. In doing so, however, we may feel some degree of jealousy and/or envy. When we experience these emotions too frequently or too intensely, they may cause problems in our trading.

The words "jealousy" and "envy" are sometimes used inter-changeably, but they refer to different emotions. People may confuse these two emotions because they frequently occur together. However, envy is the feeling you get when you want what someone else has. You feel envy when you want to make as much money on your trades as your friends or colleagues are making. Jealousy, in contrast, contains a measure of resentment. You feel jealousy when you resent the other person for having whatever it is that you envy.

People commonly feel jealousy, for example, when they believe another person has wrongfully taken something away from them, particularly when that other person is a romantic partner. Jealousy often arises when a person believes his or her lover has been receiving affection from someone else. We feel anger and resentment because we believe this other person may have wrongfully stolen the affections that belong to us.

However, it is equally possible to feel jealousy in other circumstances. For example, you may feel jealous when you are competing for a job and another person wins out over you. As "the loser," you're likely to be a little jealous of the winner. Jealousy tends to occur whenever two people are competing for a limited resource, such as first place in a contest, or profits in a stock trade. Then, it's not sufficient to want what the other has, because only one can have it. You may also feel a degree of resentment that the other person has "taken it away from you."

Most traders and investors experience envy more often than jealousy. For example, a trader may call a friend to say that he or she has just booked a big profit on a trade. Upon hearing this news, the friend may wish he had made the same trade. That is, he may envy the first trader's winning position. In moderation, envy can be a useful emotion. A successful trader may enjoy feeling envious of a successful colleague. Comparisons to other successful traders can often increase a person's motivation to do better. When you hear that another trader makes money, it is useful to think along the lines of: "If he or she can make a winning trade under these market conditions, so can I."

However, too much envy can be a problem. Pathological levels of envy can occur when a person not only desires what another person has, but feels poorly about oneself for not having the same thing. When this occurs, envy can be a symptom of a deeper problem, such as feelings of inadequacy.

Feeling jealousy too often presents even more problems (See Lazarus, 1991). Jealousy can occur when a person incorrectly believes that other people are trying to put them down, or degrade them, by bringing up their own success. Some people may compensate for feelings of jealousy by trying to make others feel inferior to them. But the better approach is to try to avoid feeling poorly about oneself.

Extreme envy and jealousy may have deep rooted causes. Psychoanalysts, including Melanie Klein (cited in Lazarus, 1991), suggest that pathological levels of jealousy may develop from childhood experiences in which the child competes with a sibling for the parents' affections. A jealous person may have had a brother or sister who seemed to be their parents' favorite, and may have grown up believing that the brother or sister unfairly received more affection from them. Similar experiences may develop in school also, where a person may have competed with a best friend for whatever seemed important at the time. If the best friend seemed to win too often, the person may have begun to feel inferior, and may have developed the belief that he or she could never win.

When this kind of "sibling rivalry" carries over into adult life, it can cause major problems. People may unnecessarily compare themselves to others, compete with them, and feel slighted or inferior whenever they lose. People who experience extreme jealousy may continuously strive for unrealistic levels of recognition, respect, and attention, and since they can never get it, spend much of their adult lives feeling wronged and hurt. These negative emotions frequently drive one into long-term unhappiness and frustration.

What do you do if you experience feelings of envy or jealousy from time to time? These negative emotions can interfere with the rational decision making you need to be successfully trading the markets. Strong feelings of envy and jealousy usually reflect a strong desire to prove your worth to yourself and to others. Left unchecked, this strong desire may lead you to take unnecessary risks.

Frequent and intense feelings of envy and jealousy can cause quite serious problems for a trader. Usually, they result from feelings of inadequacy and low self-esteem. Do you frequently compare yourself to others and try to compete with them? Are you often thinking about how others seem to be more successful than you? Do you feel that life has treated you unfairly? Does it seem to you that other people are doing better than they deserve? If your answer to any of these questions is “Yes,” then your feelings of jealousy may reflect a deep need to gain approval and acceptance.

Although it is sometimes useful to compare yourself to others, such comparisons can cause problems for people who experience intense feelings of jealousy. If you have this tendency, you’ll do better to avoid any such comparisons. Considering your own success in comparison to someone else’s will most likely reinforce your feeling that you are not doing well enough in life, and that you should be doing better. There’s very little to be gained by such thoughts and feelings, especially if you tend to feel resentful toward others, and to feel poorly about yourself.

To remedy this situation, try to develop your own internal standards of success, so that you don’t need to look toward others for what your standards should be. By avoiding comparisons with others, you will learn to appreciate the real successes you have achieved. For example, how much money you make compared to others doesn’t much matter. What really matters is that you make enough money to feel satisfied, and that you are enjoying the process of making money. If you are new to trading, consider that as you put on more trades, your skills will continue to develop. You can feel proud of these accomplishments, regardless of your current income. If you are a seasoned trader who already makes reasonable profits, you have good reason to feel proud of what you can do and what you have accomplished.

At some point, you may want to explore some of the past experiences that may have contributed to the reasons why you now feel so much envy or jealousy. Perhaps you had siblings who competed with you for your parents’ affections. Perhaps you had a significant friend, or enemy, who always seemed to put you down or make you feel beaten up. You may be carrying elements of these or other past relationships into your adult life. If so, professional psychological help may provide you with a way to explore and remove these issues.

You may also want to consider how unproductive and unrealistic intense jealousy can be in the trading environment. Feelings of envy, jealousy, and resentment tend to distract you from the focus and the calm detachment you need to trade effectively. What's more, your feelings of jealousy may drive you to discount your own accomplishments, and make whatever level of success you achieve seem inadequate and unimportant.

You should also consider how trading is different from a sibling rivalry. Siblings compete for limited resources, such as their parents' attention. In trading and investment, however, the market can provide almost limitless profits; both you and your friends can make money. This means that, just because a friend or colleague makes money, there's no reason to believe that you cannot make money also. Since there are enough profits to go around, there is no reason for you to be jealous of others.

By controlling and tempering your tendency toward jealously, you can greatly increase your effectiveness as a trader. The secret is to learn to appreciate what you have accomplished, rather than always focusing on something more.

Who's The Better Trader?

Experienced traders recognize that their psychology is often the primary determinant of their success. And psychology is a complex matter. There are many different ways it can boost your results or limit them.

One of the most insidious aspects of investment psychology is the jealousy factor: the mental and emotional comparisons you make to other traders, whether you know them personally or just hear about them. Most traders take at least some pleasure from stories of other traders who are less successful than they are, but beat themselves up when comparing themselves to traders who are more successful.

The problem is that such comparisons can dangerously inflate your self-confidence, or unfairly diminish your self-esteem. Let's face it: you're certainly a better trader than many others trying to make profitable trades. Yet even the best traders can find people who generate more income, or have profited more from a special trading opportunity.

Instead of making comparisons with others, it's far more fruitful to limit comparisons to your own past performance. Consider John Wooden, the famous UCLA basketball coach. He never talked to his team about winning. Instead, he focused their attention and effort on continuously trying to improve. His teams' unmatched winning records were a natural by-product of this approach. Or consider the highly competitive fund management industry, where performance comparisons are vitally important. A few years ago, a member of Innerworth's advisory board was talking with the manager of a multi-billion dollar hedge fund, and was surprised to discover that this trader had absolutely no idea how his fellow competitors were doing for the year, so intense was his focus on his own performance.

You can follow the lead of these winners by avoiding comparisons to others. Instead, focus on comparing your current performance to your past performance: Am I trading smarter than before? Have I increased my ratio of winners to losers? Do my trades have an improved ratio of upside to downside potential?

By sidestepping the urge to compare yourself to others, you short-circuit the dangerous emotions of jealousy and envy. The result is to keep you more accurately in touch with your strengths and weaknesses as a trader, and to set the stage for you to continuously improve your trading performance.

Envy Reduces Effectiveness

It's one of the seven deadly sins, and it can seriously degrade your effectiveness as a trader. Envy is a fairly common human emotion, and in the trading world there are certainly many people and situations that make good targets for envy. But while a little envy here and there is no problem, envy that grabs on and does not let go deserves no place in your trading day.

Trading is a difficult and demanding occupation that requires a "single point" of attention. Becoming wrapped up in envy while you trade will tend to reduce your concentration and effectiveness, because it takes you out of your trader's mind-set. It diverts energy that could and should be used to find and execute better trades.

Here are some ideas for how to replace your problem behaviors and feelings of envy with more productive ones.

Observe the envy: Be aware of your own envious feelings. Just as acknowledging a problem is the first step toward solving it, acknowledging your envy is the first step in eliminating its impact on your trading.

Postpone the envy for later: Instead of giving in to envy, try to put off those feelings until you have more time for them. Sometimes, you can even make a promise to yourself to explore certain feelings at a certain time – a time when the markets are closed.

Defuse the envy: Envy often results from too much attention turned outward. Turn your attention back inward, and you'll reap the rewards that come from concentrating on and cherishing the successes and the people in your own life.

Downgrade the envy: Envy is particularly prone to primitive emotional irrationality. We typically envy that other person's car, home, or trading track record, without recognizing that every prize carries a price tag. To weaken your envious feelings, think about other aspects of that other person's life that you don't want: his or her personality and habits, family members, work pressures, illnesses, past experiences, and all the rest. Most times, envy fades quickly when you make a realistic appraisal of another person's true situation.

Disregard the envy: You'll gain satisfaction and energy when you rise above your instincts and emotions. Since trading is not instinctual, why contaminate it with instinctual feelings? Instead, you can learn to simply disregard your feelings of envy and, with practice, let that jealousy wither away from neglect.

Gaining Mastery Over Regret

The Dynamics of Regret

Consider a tale of two brothers, Allen and Jason, who decided to go long on Home Depot last January. Although they both made the same decision, they did so for very different reasons. Allen bought stock in Home Depot because his Grandpa Ed, an experienced investor and corporate executive, thought it would be a good investment. Allen tends to blindly follow his grandfather's advice. Jason, in contrast, is much more independent and industrious. He conducted a careful analysis of buying trends, sales, profit growth, and earnings per share. He based his decision solely on his own detailed analysis.

Home Depot has been falling since March, and fell 7% last week due to stiff competition and sluggish sales. Who do you think feels more regret, Allen or Jason?

When asked this question, most people say Jason will feel more regret. Here's why. We feel regret when we engage in the wrong course of action, and put a lot of our ego on the line when taking that course. We tend to believe that Allen will feel less regret because from his point of view, he didn't have much of his ego at stake when making his decision. He just blindly followed his grandfather's advice. Rather than feel regret, he can easily accept his loss and think, "It's not my fault that I lost money on that trade, it's my grandfather's fault." Jason, in contrast, feels more regret. By putting his ego on the line, he must face the personal humiliation of having made an inaccurate forecast. He may now question his ability to conduct an accurate analysis or to develop a sound trading strategy.

Feelings of regret are painful, and people avoid them at all costs. It often seems as if the easiest way to avoid feelings of regret is to avoid making decisions. If you don't make decisions, you can't be wrong or feel regret. Right? Well, that's what a lot of people think. It's rarely true, however. Ironically, research studies have shown that when people are asked to reconsider past life decisions, the most regretful are those who either didn't make their own life decisions or merely followed the opinions of others. So it's better to take action now than regret inaction later. People's thinking tends to be faulty when it concerns regret. They think regret is painful, so they avoid making decisions to curb these feelings. However, by doing so, they have merely traded short-term immediate feelings of regret for later long-term profound feelings of regret. People who make their own decisions, based on their own opinions or beliefs, may face some regret in the short-term but over the long-term, they are more satisfied with their decisions. The immediate experience of regret is much less painful than we think it will be. Long-term feelings of regret due to inaction are more enduring.

Don't let the tendency to avoid regret influence your trading decisions. Keep in mind that if a decision leads to an unpleasant consequence, you may feel a little regret, but you can handle it. It's better to make mistakes, and experience a little temporary regret now, than a lot of profound regret later.

Seeking Pride and Avoiding Regret

Jason has been holding a position in Dell Computer for the past month. It's been doing well so far, and earnings forecasts suggest profits, in part due to sales in new markets. On the other hand, economic figures seem grim. The business news is full of stories of company cutbacks, which can easily suggest lower sales for new computers. Jason is stuck in a quandary. He's proud of his decision to buy Dell, and he's hoping to make a profitable trade, but he wonders, "Am I trading on the news? Am I listening to the media and ignoring other more important economic indicators? Should I sell now or hold it a little longer?" He wants to make a profit, but on the other hand, he doesn't want his winning position to turn into a loser. It's one thing to make a wrong guess upon opening a position, it's quite another to let a winning trade turn into a loser. Inaction is a major cause of regret. Rather than face that possible regret, why not just sell now, lock in the profits, and feel pride?

The interplay between regret and pride influences many investment decisions. On the one hand, people prefer to experience pride, and bask in the glory of a winning trade, but on the other hand, "they need to let their winning trades run." Letting a winning trade run is hard to do. It's possible that it will turn around, and the inaction of holding the position may cause regret later.

According to behavioral economists, regret and pride are the two most pervasive and powerful emotions when it comes to investment decisions (Shefrin, 2000). Traders and investors seek out pride and avoid regret. Pride is experienced when we have accomplished an important goal. It results in a feeling of extreme pleasure. Regret occurs when we have made a poor decision. According to behavioral economists, the need for pride and avoidance of regret work together to make traders and investors prematurely sells off winning positions and hold losers unnecessarily. Here's how it works. Selling a loser forces investors to acknowledge that their trading plan was flawed. Instead of feeling pride, they feel ashamed, which is an unpleasant emotion. It's hard to face regret from making a bad decision, so such a decision is put off. By leaving the losses on paper, the feelings of shame and regret are avoided. On the other hand, selling a winning position allows for bragging rights. A person can feel the pride of making a big win, and bask in the glory of a good trade. What's wrong with this strategy? Winning positions are likely to remain winning positions. If a trader could hold onto the winning position, then it would have made additional profits. By selling it early, to feel a sense of pride, the investor feels good at the expense of a greater profit. In addition, since the position is usually held less than one year, capital gains taxes must be paid. Selling losing positions would be a much wiser move. Losing positions tend to fall even farther in the future, and there are tax advantages for closing them. Don't let regret and pride get the best of you. Sell your losers and keep your winners.

Managing Guilt

People feel guilty when they believe they have broken a moral imperative. Everyone has his or her own values, which he or she holds dear. Guilt is the quick and dirty way our psyche tells us we have broken an important moral value (Lazarus, 1991). The easiest way to eliminate guilt is to change your moral convictions. A common belief among novice traders is that the money they invest trading is better spent on more sound investments that may ensure the future security of their family. If you hold this belief, you must decide for yourself whether you believe this to be the case. By questioning and refuting this belief, you will feel less guilty. That is, if you can convince yourself that spending money trading does not unnecessarily risk the financial security of your family, then you will not feel as guilty.

But merely questioning this assertion without a strong basis in reality isn't a good idea. Don't fool yourself into believing that a moral belief you truly believe is actually false. If you truly view your family's security as an important value to you, for example, it is not a good idea to question it. You must find another alternative. One may justify his or her trading by thinking, "I'm not risking my family's financial security because I'm going to make a lot of money through trading." If you make such a rationalization, you better be quite certain that you can follow through. Few people can make such a claim when they first start trading. In all likelihood, novice traders tend to lose a lot more money than they make. One should expect to lose money, rather than make it. So if you can't afford to lose money, and cannot also preserve your family's security through some other means, it is simply not a good idea to continue trading. In this case, your feelings of guilt are protecting you from doing something you really do not want to do.

If trading means that you will risk the security of your family, then you must not use that money to trade. If you do, you will continue to feel guilty, and you will probably be placing a great deal of pressure on yourself to perform. Such extreme pressure may be your undoing. Most people "blow out" their account completely under such pressure.

The best solution is to find a compromise. Develop a financial plan for ensuring a basic sense of security for your family, then make sacrifices in other areas of your personal budget so that you can build up a trading fund. View this fund as disposable in that you can literally afford to lose all of it without the loss hurting your lifestyle. It's better to put off active trading until you build up this trading account. Once you build it up, you can trade it carefully, and use it to hone your trading skills. You will find that you no longer feel guilty when you lose money, and in the long run, you can develop the carefree trading approach associated with successful trading.

Dealing with Loss

The Will to Get Out

One of the most important differences between top traders and the rest of the investing crowd is how they handle losers, particularly with reference to making quick exits. Once a position turns unprofitable, the average investor hems and haws, thinks about getting out or staying in, evaluates the options, and more often than not simply postpones a decision on what to do about this losing position. The top trader barely rethinks the situation, if it all, and most times gets out as automatically as flipping out the lights when leaving a room. These behavioral differences are practical reflections of the top traders' will to leave losing positions behind as quickly and inexpensively as possible. The will to leave losing positions behind involves several critical elements:

In-depth knowledge of your trading method: Too many losers may signal that your trading method is starting to fall out of touch with the markets. Unless you are very well versed in how and why your trading method works, however, trades that go against you may not raise any red flags. This is a serious problem. Every losing trade should be considered, at least from time to time, as you reevaluate your trading method and check that it continues to be useful.

Recognition that losses are very damaging: Trading is a privilege that requires investment capital. Every lost dollar brings you closer to the day when your account is depleted and you can no longer trade. Successful traders know it is better to take many small losses and stay in the game than to risk big losses that can force them out of the markets for a long period of time.

Enough self-confidence to accept losses without fear or pain: Run-of-the-mill traders often have a confidence problem, and cannot easily accept the fact of another losing trade. So they hang on, hoping for a reversal. Top traders, however, have plenty of confidence in themselves and their trading method. Their emotional comfort is not threatened by taking a loss, particularly a small one. This strategy allows them to find more opportunities to build their confidence by placing winning trades.

Recovering From a Bad Day

Every trader inevitably experiences one or more bad days when trades do not go as expected, when unusual events or market dynamics interfere with normally safe trades, or when illness or personal problems reduce the accuracy of their decision-making. No matter how hard you work or how smart you are, there will always be some factors beyond your control that go haywire from time to time and knock your trading effectiveness for a loop. So what can you do? Since eliminating all your bad days is a practical impossibility, the next best remedy is to be sure you handle those inevitable bad days as professionally and positively as possible. For example, next time you have a bad trading day, make sure you:

Recognize the problem early: In retrospect, it is easy to see which days your trading was red hot, and which days it was cold. But retrospective judgments are not good enough, because by then your losses are final and the damage is done. You must identify and stay on the alert for signals that help you spot a bad day as early as possible.

Establish a circuit-breaker to stop you from trading: The simplest method for abandoning the market on a bad day is to establish a daily maximum for losses. When you hit your limit, stop placing trades. But if you do not want such strict, objective limits on your trading, you can monitor how sharply you are executing your trades, or how you are feeling, or even how accurately you are projecting market action. If you are not trading with your usual clarity and acumen, stop trading for the day.

Have a recovery plan: As important as getting out of the market is for facilitating your recovery, so is having a plan for how you can get back in and start winning again. The key is to know which activities rejuvenate your spirits, your energy, and your positive state of mind. Consider going for a long walk, getting busy in your garden, playing sports, reading for relaxation, or just catching up with your family. Develop your own recovery plan, so after your next bad day, you can rapidly re-enter the market.

Sense when you are back in form: Resuming your trading too soon is only a little better than continuing to trade; in both cases you will continue to deplete your account balance. To prevent throwing good money after bad, find a reliable indicator, such as your ability to laugh at a joke, to smile at yourself in the mirror, or to see clear patterns in the charts to help you know when you are fully recovered and ready to resume trading on a positive note.

Chapter 7

Biases in Decision Making

"Cut your losses and let your profits run" is a commonly heard adage, but it is often easier said than done. Many times, when people find themselves in situations where they are losing money, they persist with a losing course of action, rather than cut their losses. In fact, there are many instances where people increase their commitment and are willing to feed an investment in order to sustain it. Trading coaches have been aware of this phenomenon for quite some time, but recently, scholars have been interested in explaining such behavior. In the emerging field of behavioral finance, researchers have used social psychological and cognitive information processing approaches to explain why people are risk averse when faced with conditions of uncertainty. One of the most influential people in this area is Daniel Kahenman, a psychologist who won the 2002 Nobel Prize in Economics. In this chapter, we present some essays about this relatively new academic field. We've tried to explain the findings from scientific studies in clear everyday language without jargon or unnecessary complexity. The chapter begins with a summary of the work by Dr. Barry Staw. He's not in the field of behavioral finance, but he has written a series of articles on the reasons for why people persist in losing courses of action. I've adapted and extended his model to trading and investing. The description of this adapted model provides an overview of the basic psychological and social processes that influence traders who have trouble cutting losses, and outlines the various theories behavioral economists use to study why traders and investors prematurely sell off winning trades and hold on to losers.

Unwarranted Persistence

Researchers, such as Professor Barry Staw at the Haas Business School, University of California, Berkeley, have studied the social and psychological factors that may explain why people persist in failing courses of action (Staw & Ross, 1987; 1989). You may be aware of some of these factors, but it is worth reviewing them.

Certainty of the loss: People tend to increase their commitment to losing courses of action when the outcomes are viewed as uncertain. For example, research studies have shown that when investors believe that the loss is only temporary and that over time, a losing investment will turn a profit, they hold on to the investment and even add more money to the investment to keep it going. However, when people perceive that losses will continue to mount if the investment is maintained, they close out the investment.

Thus, sound decision-making requires that the possible outcomes of an investment always be at the forefront. If the possible outcomes of an investment are left vague or unclear, one may have the strong tendency to assume that the outcomes are uncertain, temporary, and changeable. Acting on these beliefs, one is likely to continue to hold on to a losing investment. To counteract this tendency, it is essential to always carefully outline each possible outcome and arrive at a realistic estimate of its likelihood.

Even if one decides to hold on to a losing investment, it is important to look at how much one has lost and decide whether it is realistic to expect the investment to turn around. For example, it is possible that the market may be at a temporary low point, and that some recent news will turn the market around, such as an anticipation that interest rates will be lowered. If you realistically believe that the market will change, it is reasonable to hold on to the investment to see what happens next. However, be sure that you are not taking an unnecessary risk. Are you certain that a decrease in price is due to temporary circumstances? Don't fool yourself into believing something that isn't true. Set a limit as to how long you will wait before market conditions move in your favor. If that time limit is met, and conditions still have not changed, it is best to close out the position.

Sunk costs: People tend to believe that an investment is worth what they paid for it. They believe that the original purchase price endures, even when market prices suggest that the value has decreased. Sunk costs refer to the amount that is paid to acquire a stock or commodity. Sunk costs increase when the value of the stock or commodity decreases. Sound decision-making requires that one base decisions on current values, rather than past values. Research has shown that people tend to keep an investment when the sunk costs are high; that is, when they have lost a lot of money on a trade. They tend to believe that the value is higher than the market suggests, and believe that the "true" value is closer to their initial cost, or entry point, rather than its current value. But this isn't well founded. The value is what the market places on it, regardless of the original purchase price.

When sunk costs are high, people can also tend to be fatalistic. They believe that since they have lost a large amount of money, they have very little to lose if they wait to see what happens next. It's like thinking, "I've lost so much already, what else do I have to lose?" This is a psychological tendency you must avoid. You could lose your entire investment, and psychologically, you could experience a lot of stress holding on to a losing trade. There are real financial and psychological costs for refusing to ignore sunk costs. It is better to evaluate the potential of a trade based on what you can make in the future and assume that you will not be able to recoup what you have lost. If you cannot see how the trade can turn itself around, cut your losses. You will reduce your psychological and financial costs in the long run.

Framing effects: People tend to seek out risks when faced with losses. You may have seen a common decision making exercise in which you are given two alternatives: (a) a sure loss of $100 or (b) a 10% chance of losing $1000. People prefer to take a chance of losing $1000, when faced with a losing trade. They tend to be willing to gamble with a loss, yet are afraid to gamble with their wins. For example, they would take a sure win of $100 over a 10% chance of winning $1000.

The tendency to take risks when facing a loss may cause people to hold on to a losing trade. People impulsively believe that by taking a chance, the odds will work in their favor and produce a win. This is a poor way to make decisions, and it is important to be aware of this tendency. People naturally seek out risks when facing a losing trade, so you must make sure that you have clearly defined exit strategies that you can follow, and avoid this decision-making bias.

Illusions of control: Other psychological factors correlated with unwarranted persistence are more dynamic. One of these is an unrealistic illusion of control. Many people believe they can beat the markets. They are aware that it is difficult to turn a losing trade around and that the odds are not in the trader's favor. Yet they believe they are special and that they have special talents or good fortune that can turn a losing trade into a winner. This belief is dangerous. No one is protected from poor odds or a run of bad luck. It is important to be aware of the tendency to be overly optimistic. Control this tendency.

Self-justifications: People's attitudes and beliefs are often shaped by the decisions they make. Once we make a decision, we tend to change our beliefs to be consistent with that decision. Psychologists have shown in experimental studies that no matter what decision is made, people tend to believe they made the right decision, and unconsciously change their attitudes in order to have attitudes that are consistent with their decisions. Thus, when you make an investment decision, you believe you made the right choice and tend to search for evidence to support that decision. The search for evidence is often biased in that you may focus on information that supports your decision while ignoring evidence that does not support your decision.

It is hard to fight this tendency. But it is important to be aware of it, and realize that it will impact how you feel about a trade, and subsequent decision making. Since we know the human tendency is to seek out confirming information, it is important to seek out disconfirming information. But even this may not work. This tendency is strong and difficult to overcome. Realize that you may be too involved with your investment to make an informed decision. It may be necessary to find an advisor who is more objective, and can help you evaluate your alternatives.

Security and identity: Another reason people hold on to a losing investment concerns the consequence of admitting losses. Sometimes, investors are afraid to close out a position because doing so means admitting that a significant amount of trading capital has been lost. The loss may be so large that it means that the investor can no longer trade, or it may mean the investor has to work for many years to recover the losses. In these cases, it is easier to hold on to the trade and keep the losses on paper, rather than close out the position, and actually face the losses. However, this approach can only make matters worse in the long run. The investor will continue to lose money and incur even greater losses. One way to minimize the impact of this factor in decision making is to use proper risk management, so that any given trade is a relatively small amount of trading capital.

Social factors may also play a role in failing to acknowledge losses. Investors who work for financial institutions may be afraid to admit to their superiors or clients that they have made an investment or series of investments that have resulted in losses. In an unconscious attempt to save face, investors may want to hide the loss. This social factor can also occur for an individual investor, if he or she has a social network of friends, and believes that he or she may face humiliation upon admitting a loss. It is important to admit losses no matter what the social consequences. You will have to face the consequences sooner or later, so you might as well face them sooner than later. When the losses have mounted, it will be even more difficult to face the consequences.

Fame and glory: In our society, a strong business leader is one who is viewed as a person who persists in hard times and beats the odds. People who persistently strive to overcome impossible odds to become successful are viewed as heroes in the business community. These beliefs and expectations may push people to persist in a losing trade. One may believe that by turning the losing trade around, it will prove that he or she is a superior trader. However, it is difficult to turn a losing trade around. This kind of persistence is risky and should be avoided. The kind of persistence that is appropriate to trading concerns continuing to put on trades even though past trades have lost. It concerns persistence after a continuous string of loses, rather than persisting with a single losing trade.

Decision-Making Biases: A Primer

Our common-sense approach to decision making often works quite well, but there are times when we arrive at decisions that are just plain wrong. This has led some psychologists, such as Amos Tversky and Daniel Kahneman (1973), to suggest that everyday thinking departs from "rationality." That is, compared to an ideal rational decision-making machine that only analyzes and interprets hard data, humans extend their knowledge beyond the limits. They don't have the hard facts or actual data in front of them at all times, so under these circumstances, they rely on "heuristics" or "rules of thumb" to make decisions.

Let's look at some classic examples to understand how these everyday rules of thumb or heuristics work. Consider two questions that most people do not have the actual data for use as a basis for making judgments:

1. Which is more likely in the English language?

(A) Words beginning with the letter K (such as *kind*)
(B) Words with K as the third letter (such as *make*)

2. Upon visiting the Middle East, which situation are you more likely to encounter?

(A) Terrorist attack
(B) Traffic accident

When research participants are asked these two questions, they are more likely to choose selection (A) as the correct answer. Why? Tversky and Kahneman note that we do not have the actual data in front of us to use as a basis for answering these questions. Instead, we must rely on our memories. When it comes to words in the English language, we do not know off hand how many words begin with K versus how many have K as the third letter. Thus, we try to think of examples. It's easy to think of words that begin with K, but it is much harder to think of words where K is the third letter. Most people believe that more words begin with K than have K in the third position based solely on the ability to recall instances. But this does not produce the correct answer. Many more words have K in the third position. It's just hard to recall them. (It's even hard to list examples using a dictionary.)

People answer the second question using a similar approach. We can easily recall vivid instances of terrorist attacks in the Middle East (especially these days), and so we believe there are more terrorist attacks than traffic accidents in the Middle East. The hard data, however, show that more traffic accidents occur than terrorist attacks. Again, our memory fools us. We rely on our memory to provide data, rather than knowing that we should not trust our memory and seek out the actual hard data for our judgments.

Tversky and Kahneman (1973) call this phenomenon the *availability heuristic*. Certain memories of events are more easily recalled, and thus, are more "available" for use in making decisions. In many everyday situations, using the available information is all we can do. It works as a decision-making strategy much of the time, but we have to remember that there are some situations where we don't have all the necessary hard data to make a decision. It's at these times that we need to tediously find the actual data and use it as a basis for making decisions. Behavioral economists have been very persuaded by the work of Tversky and Kahneman. Economists have had difficulty making accurate forecasts of the market, and behavioral economists are interested in finding examples of "irrational decisions" to explain why market prices are difficult to predict. It's useful to consider this perspective. Perhaps some of the decisions you make are "irrational" and should be avoided. Look out for them!

Behavioral Finance: A More Credible Field

Research studies from the emerging field of behavioral finance emphasize the influence of psychology in investment decisions. In contrast to traditional finance and economics, which try to look only at concrete indicators in an attempt to make accurate economic forecasts, behavioral economists assume that forecasts are prone to inaccuracy. People make forecasts and people are fallible; they are "irrational" in that they don't base their decisions on a logical analysis of all available information. Instead, they use "rules of thumb" and shortcuts. The use of these shortcuts often produces inaccurate predictions. According to behavioral economists, it's because people use these shortcuts that stock prices are more of a reflection of "investor psychology" than traditional fundamental indicators. The work of Daniel Kahneman has influenced many behavioral economists. In several illuminating experiments, Dr. Kahneman, and his late colleague Amos Tversky, demonstrated that humans are risk averse and inefficient processors of information. They make quick and dirty decisions rather than ones based on careful logic. Some of the heuristics that have been applied to the understanding of the markets are the availability heuristic (believing a stock or sector will go up in price because it is easy to recall past instances from memory) and the representiveness heuristic (if a stock has characteristics that are similar to a kind of stock that usually goes up, then it will go up).

From the vantage point of a psychologist, it is not surprising that economists have had difficultly making accurate market forecasts: Investors' behavior is hard to predict. Psychologists, such as Clark Hull, tried to predict behavior in the 1940s and found they could not. Since then, they have known that it's difficult to predict people's behavior, and thus, the financial markets. But what have economists been trying to do? It seems as if economists have been fruitlessly trying to develop complex mathematical models to predict the markets. Many people believe it is possible to develop such models, and at the same time, view investment psychology as on the periphery, misguided, or a little "New Agey." If you think that, consider this: psychologist Daniel Kahneman recently won the 2002 Nobel Prize for Economics. Perhaps winning the award may not change the minds of some folks who just find psychology full of "psychobabble." And winning a Nobel Prize doesn't prove the validity of a theory (Remember Scholes and Merton's involvement in Long Term Capital Management). But perhaps more people will consider the findings from investment psychology and behavioral finance more seriously. We hope they will.

Sunk Costs

You've invested 25% of your capital in a stock that your analysis had predicted would increase. Your expectations haven't been supported, however. The price has been steadily declining. You think, "I did such a careful and detailed analysis. I've spent a lot of time studying the fundamentals of this company. I can't believe it's going down." At this point, you may hope that the position will reverse, and refuse to close it out. It's easier to keep it open than accept the loss and feel the regret of making a bad decision. This is called the *sunk cost effect*: A person increases one's commitment to a losing position because a great deal of time, effort, and/or money has been spent.

The most obvious and blatant example of the sunk cost effect is when we have invested a large percentage of our capital in a losing position and we don't want to admit that we have lost what we have invested. There are other more subtle ways of experiencing the sunk cost effect, however. Most people don't consider them, but they may still influence investment decisions.

The old adage "time is money" illustrates another way that one can "lose money." Just putting time and effort into an investment is a way of spending money. For example, let's say that you study a particular company closely. You read reports on the fundamentals of the company, and you follow the stock price on a daily basis, noting price changes that correspond to company announcements and significant events in the industry. The more effort you expend on preparation and analysis, the greater the sunk costs you will experience. There is a strong tendency to justify the time and effort you have expended. Why spend so much time and effort studying this company if you don't plan to invest in it? This tendency to want to justify your behavior will gnaw at you, and if you are not aware of it, and are not trying to control it, you will have a tendency to want to invest (long or short) in the stock, even when you know you should stay out and wait for another opportunity. It's useful to be aware of this subtle effect. Ask yourself, "Do I want to invest because I see a real opportunity or am I merely trying to justify the amount of effort I've put in?" It's important to be aware of how this subtle yet powerful influence can lead you to make a decision you will regret later.

Overcoming this subtle influence is difficult. It's a good idea to study companies closely and capitalize on an opportunity when one arises, but don't overdo it. Remember that expending too much effort has a subtle impact. Try to overcome it. Remind yourself that you don't have to invest. Your study and preparation will pay off big someday, but learn to wait for the right opportunity.

Be aware of both the subtle and blatant ways that the sunk cost effect can influence your behavior. Try to consider whether or not sunk costs are influencing your decisions. Try to rationally counteract them, and prevent them from getting the best of you.

What Will They Think?

You're in the mood to indulge yourself. You go to the supermarket and fill your basket with soda, chips, candy bars, ice cream, and cookies. As the cashier scans your items, you think, "This cashier must think I'm a pig; look at all the junk food I'm buying." When interacting with others, it's natural to consider how you'll be perceived. In order to avoid being perceived negatively, people will tend to curb or change their activities. There is a natural tendency to do what is socially acceptable, even if it means putting your needs and desires on hold.

When trading, many traders can't help but feel as if they're being watched or their actions followed. There's that same natural inclination to behave in a socially acceptable way. There are many social interactions when it comes to stock trading. When you buy shares of a stock, you're buying them from someone, and there are people on the exchange floors matching your bids and asks. When one considers the social interactions involved in trading, he or she may experience the same type of concerns as the shopper buying too much junk food. The trader thinks, "I don't want to look stupid. I don't want to look like a moron." He or she might not explicitly say this, but experience the associated feelings, nevertheless. This can then lead to last-minute hesitation, loss of risk control, and other undesirable behaviors, which will lead to losses, both in terms of capital and self-confidence.

It's useful to gain awareness of the need to act in a socially desirable manner and curb it. The shopper buying junk food need not worry about the cashier's opinion. He or she may have served more than a hundred people that day and probably didn't notice or care how much junk food the shopper purchased. Similarly, if traders try to identify specific points of interaction between themselves and others, they will quickly realize that the human interaction, if there is one, is of little consequence. Even the brokerage firm doesn't look specifically at a single trader's statements or even care.

In many walks of life, and in several professions, it's prudent to carefully study social interactions. Social blunders can have dire consequences for one's career. But when it comes to trading, they are of no consequence. It doesn't matter what a broker thinks. It doesn't matter what other traders think of your strategy, and most of the time, they don't even care. Considering what others think can only hinder your trading. It puts on unnecessary pressure. If you find yourself feeling as if you are being watched and that others are evaluating you, stop. Remind yourself that when it comes to trading, it doesn't matter. All that matters is your ability to think independently. And that means not caring what anyone else thinks.

If P, Then Q

If asked to evaluate the truth of the statement, "If you traded MSFT during the month of May, you made a profit," most people would start the process of evaluation by trying to think of people who traded MSFT during May and made a profit. And after coming up with one or more examples, they would evaluate the statement as being true. In other words, they would immediately look for confirming evidence. But if there was even one person who traded MSFT during May and did not make a profit (even if the evaluator didn't know of this person), he or she would probably decide the statement was false.

The logical way of evaluating any proposition is to look for evidence that confirms or disconfirms it; in this case, one may ask, "Who traded MSFT in May and didn't make a profit?" If you can think of even one example, you've disconfirmed it and know it's false.

A common decision-making bias is to evaluate the validity of a proposition by searching for confirming evidence. Disconfirming evidence, however, is more useful. It's vital to search for disconfirming evidence when making decisions. A failure to do so can be an especially serious impediment to trading success. One is constantly evaluating trading plans, technical signals and indicators and news. Studying this information in an objective and logical way is vital to trading success. It's important to seek out disconfirming evidence.

Suppose you've developed a technical analysis method that you believe will give you excellent indicators. If you backtest this method by only looking for cases where it works, it's possible that you'll identify 10 instances where it works just as you expected. But there may be 500 instances where your method did not work. These disconfirming instances are far more important, and you cannot ignore them. Through your biased evaluation, you will conclude that your method is very effective, but in fact, you will set yourself up to be overconfident about it.

Traders tend to be particularly vulnerable to this difficulty in evaluation because they're usually evaluating trading plans or methods they think might yield them great profits. They naturally want to confirm their positive expectations, thus pushing them even further to look for confirming evidence.

When evaluating a theory or statement, it helps to play devil's advocate: try to come up with a proof for why the theory or statement is false. Be objective. Evaluate an issue from multiple perspectives before arriving at a final conclusion.

Confirmation Bias

A common decision-making bias that influences traders' decisions is called "confirmation bias." Suppose you decided to go long on Stock A.

	High	Low	Close	Change From Yesterday
Stock A	75.75	73.21	75.65	+1.84

In evaluating your decision, suppose you also decided to look at two additional stocks, B and C, that are strongly correlated with Stock A.

	High	Low	Close	Change From Yesterday
Stock B	65.20	64.10	64.90	+1.91
Stock C	72.10	65.20	61.20	-2.19

Which information would you find more useful? Most people tend to pick the information for Stock B. It confirms the decision to go long on Stock A. This tendency to seek out confirming evidence is known as "confirmation bias." People tend to seek out information that supports their decision while discounting information that contradicts it.

Actually, since both Stock B and Stock C are strongly correlated with Stock A, the information provided by the price action of Stock C is much more valuable than that of Stock B. Stock C contradicts the decision to go long. People tend not to give the appropriate amount of weight to disconfirming evidence. Instead, they view such evidence as an anomaly. In fact, they should give it more weight than confirming evidence.

When making price forecasts, it is vital that you consider the tendency to seek out confirming evidence. Seek out signals and indicators that may contradict your decision. It's easy to consider information that supports your decision; it's hard to consider information that contradicts it. If you can learn to find disconfirming evidence, you will have an edge over other traders.

Insufficient Justification

A common problem among traders and investors is the tendency to sell profitable trades prematurely and hold losing trades unnecessarily. Once we have held a losing trade for a long time, we have a strong need to justify our actions. This need for justification is so powerful that we often change our opinions because of it. We start to believe that the losing trade will turn around, rather than admit we have spent money and psychological effort for no good reason. This is called the *insufficient justification effect.*

A classic study in social psychology illustrates the powerful impact insufficient justification has on opinions. Research participants were asked to complete a very boring 1-hour task in which they had to look at pictures and make decisions about them. After completing the task, all participants agreed it was boring. Participants were then persuaded to recruit other participants for the task. They were asked to give a "hard sell" in which they described how fun and interesting the boring task was. Half of the participants were given $1 for making the sales pitch while half were given $200. After delivering the sales pitch, all participants were again asked to rate how interesting they thought the task was. People given $200 didn't change their minds. They still thought the task was boring. People given $1, in contrast, changed their minds; they thought the task was more interesting than they had previously thought. This finding shows the insufficient justification effect.

People have a strong need to maintain consistency between their beliefs and actions. When there is a discrepancy, or *cognitive dissonance*, something must change for consonance to be restored. In this case, since participants had already made the sales pitch, they couldn't change their inconsistent actions, they had to change their opinions. They thought, "I did the sales pitch in which I argued that a very boring task was interesting for only $1. Why did I do that? That doesn't make sense. I guess the task was not as boring as I had thought." People are motivated to align their beliefs and actions. Participants who were paid $200 didn't have to justify their inconsistent actions. They argued that the boring task was interesting because they were paid sufficiently to do so.

The psychological processes of logical consistency and dissonance reduction influence trading decisions as well. If one holds a losing trade for a long time, for example, one may think, "I have held this trade for a long time yet it is losing money. Why am I doing that? Why have I expended so much money and psychological energy? I must truly believe it is going to turn around." There is a strong need to justify our actions. It's especially difficult when we put our self-esteem on the line, such as when we also think, "If I admit I'm wrong, I'm a bad trader. I have to hold on to this trade." To maintain logical consistency and reduce cognitive dissonance, you must hold on to the losing trade. One way to combat this tendency is to accept a set of beliefs that will allow you to sell your position, such as, "A good trader cuts losses and I'm a good trader" or "Many times my trading strategy will fail and I must cut my losses before I make them worse." It's also useful to realize that it is difficult to take action in the midst of a losing trade. Some trading coaches suggest having a clearly defined exit strategy, such as a stop loss point, as a preventative measure. Once you engage in self-justification for holding onto a losing trade, it's hard to beat it. By taking a preventative measure, you can close out the losing trade before self-justification processes take hold. It's useful to consider the insufficient justification effect. There may be times when you engage in poor decisions to justify your actions or to maintain your self-image. Try to identify these times and try to combat them.

Actions Can Bias Opinions

"Actions speak louder than words" is a common saying that we usually apply to others. Some people say one thing, but do another. Most people tend to believe that a person's true intentions are reflected in one's actions, despite what one voices as his or her actual intentions. There is scientific evidence that we also tend to apply this saying to our own behavior as well as others. For example, if you hold the belief that vanilla ice cream is bland and unexciting compared to more exotic flavors, you will tend to avoid vanilla ice cream. But suppose someone convinced you to try vanilla ice cream and you liked it. Imagine having dinner in an expensive restaurant with friends and deciding to yield to the group pressure of having a scoop of gourmet French vanilla ice cream made in-house. Not only do you eat it, you also pay a premium for it. You would probably eat it, and you would probably like it, somewhat. Research has shown that you would also tend to change your opinion of vanilla ice cream. There is a strong human tendency to maintain "logical consistency" among our behaviors, attitudes and beliefs. Because you ate the vanilla ice cream, and spent a lot of money for it, it's logical to start believing that you must have liked it. Your prior attitudes would be changed by your actions. That is, actions speak louder than words. Thus, the easiest way to change a person's belief is to get that person to behave in a way that is opposite to his or her prior beliefs.

Another everyday influence of actions influencing our beliefs concerns consumer behavior. When shopping for a new car, have you ever noticed that once you make your decision, you tend to prefer your choice? For example, you may have had trouble deciding between a white car and a silver car while in the dealership, but once you drive the car off of the lot, you prefer whatever choice you made. You justify it. You say, "I think I made a pretty good choice." You may also start to notice how many other cars on the road are of the same color, which further demonstrates how correct you were in your decision-making.

These psychological processes also work when making investment decisions, and it is important to be aware of them. Once you commit yourself to a specific course of action, there is a strong tendency to justify your decision. This *justification bias* can distort incoming information that suggests you should change your course of action. The amount of justification you make depends on several factors. You are especially biased when your decision is explicit and unambiguous, irrevocable and hard to undo, made with a high degree of volition, important to you, and made in public. The justification bias is powerful, but can be neutralized. The more you are aware of it, the less impact it will have on your decision-making processes. So gain awareness of it, not only in your trading decisions, but in other areas of your life. Notice how your attitudes, beliefs, and opinions change after you take decisive action. Determine how much your actions speak louder than your words.

Preconceptions Can Bias Decisions

When making a prediction of whether a stock price will increase or decrease, do you weigh all possible information equally or are you sometimes swayed by a company's image? Prudent decision-making requires the thorough consideration of all objective facts, but decision-making is often biased by our preexisting attitudes and images. Sometimes, we view certain sectors or commodities as "hot" or "up and coming," and we may base our predictions on these attitudes, rather than on concrete facts and logic.

The recent dot-com bubble illustrates the disadvantage of using a company's image to make forecasts. Many investors forecasted extreme growth of stocks in this sector. Decisions were based on the image of dot-coms having extreme growth potential, rather than specific facts, such as the actual sales or earnings of the dot-com companies.

MacGregor, Slovic, and Dreman (2000) conducted a study to illustrate how preconceptions and images of stock sectors can bias price forecasts. A group of advanced business students enrolled in a securities analysis course was asked to make decisions regarding a set of industry groups on the New York Stock Exchange. Examples of the industry groups were computer software, pharmaceuticals, railroads, and managed care. Unknown to the participants, half of the industry groups consisted of high performing stocks (greater than a 20% return) while the other half consisted of low performing stocks. Participants rated each industry group on whether they had a positive (for example, value, activity, and strength) versus negative image. They were also asked to predict the rate of return for each industry group.

Analysis indicated that industry groups rated more positively were predicted to have the highest return. However, a company's image had no relation to actual market performance, as measured by weighted average returns for the industry group. In other words, participants allowed their beliefs that a particular industry group had an "image" of strength, growth, and profit to bias their forecasts.

This study shows how attitudes, beliefs and preconceptions have a powerful influence on our decisions. People have a tendency to form strong opinions about which stocks or commodities will grow in value. Many times, these opinions are based on nothing more than an "image" or gut feeling.

Don't let your preconceived images bias your price forecasts. Be aware that, sometimes, you may have a positive image of a company that may override your logic. Try to minimize the influence of these attitudes. Double-check your facts. Question the assumptions on which your trading strategies are based. Make sure that your decision to enter a trade is based on solid ground, rather than "images" or unfounded expectations.

Mere Exposure Effects and Judgment

A somewhat counterintuitive finding in the scientific literature is called the *mere exposure effect*, coined by Dr. Robert Zajonc, a social psychologist at Stanford University. The more frequently people see a stimulus, the more they like it, even if they are unaware of how familiar they are with the stimulus. The finding that mere exposure is related to a preference for the stimulus has been replicated in several studies. It doesn't seem to matter what the stimulus is. People have shown the effect when evaluating photographs of strangers, novel paintings, political candidates, and selections of classical music. The results are always the same: the more exposure or familiarity people have with an object, the more they like it. The effect occurs even when the actual frequency of exposure occurs below a person's awareness.

Although mere exposure effects have been observed in several scientific experiments, the reasons for the effect are still under debate. One plausible explanation is that familiar surroundings are associated with safety and security, and so, humans have a natural inclination to prefer objects that have been associated with safety and security in the past. Mere exposure effects are most powerful when people are in situations where no clear alternatives exist, and they doubt their ability to resolve the situation.

Many times, traders find themselves in situations where they are uncertain of an outcome. For example, they must decide which stocks or commodities to purchase, and they must decide whether the price will increase or decrease. Studies of traders have shown that mere exposure effects sometimes influence these decisions. Merely being shown particular stocks increases people's preferences for them. There are many opportunities for traders to become exposed to, or shallowly familiar, with a stock without really knowing much about it. The media may have profiled a company or stock frequently or a trader may have inadvertently come across the same stocks or commodities while doing research. Rather than a true familiarity and knowledge of the facts, traders may develop a positive attitude toward the stock or commodity merely because they have been repeatedly exposed to it over and over again. Acting on this "hunch" is a bias that must be prevented.

Be aware that your decision-making may be influenced by factors outside of your awareness. If you have a hunch that a stock or commodity is going to increase in value, it may only be an example of a "mere exposure effect." Double-check your facts. Make sure that you have several indicators that suggest a price increase. Avoid acting on a hunch.

The Law of Large Numbers

You've just put on a trade with a new method that you have been studying for the past month. It hasn't worked on the two trades you executed yesterday, and you are a little unsure of whether it will work today. You wonder, "Does this method actually work or have I fallen for the latest untested fad?" You seriously consider closing the trade and finding a new method.

Maybe you don't want to give up just yet, however. Have you given the new method a fair chance? You must test new methods on a sufficient number of occasions before making a decision as to whether they will produce a profit. However, people have a tendency to base such decisions on one or two instances, rather than a sufficient number.

Determining whether a new method will produce a profit is similar to how pollsters measure opinions in a political contest. Suppose you wanted to know the percentage of people who would vote for a candidate in an upcoming election. Would you base your estimate on only one sample? There is a human tendency to want to do so, but the consequences may be disastrous. Perhaps you have seen the erroneous 1948 newspaper headline, "Dewey Defeats Truman." A Chicago newspaper had taken a telephone poll that indicated Dewey would defeat Truman by a healthy margin. Based on this single sample, the newspaper went with the incorrect headline. The sample was inadequate in that it was small and biased. (In 1948, Dewey supporters were more likely to have a telephone than Truman supporters and the newspaper was struggling to meet a deadline, so they went with the incorrect headline under pressure to get the paper out.)

Prematurely abandoning a trading method based on only a few experiences is similar. The outcome of each trade is a sample of all possible samples from a population of trading outcomes. Due to "sampling error," a single sample may be biased. It is necessary to test a trading strategy on many "samples," that is, on many trades. But people don't believe in the law of large numbers, which is that many samples are needed to arrive at an accurate estimate. They believe that the law of large numbers applies to small numbers. A statistician will tell you, however, an estimate based on many samples is more reliable than one based on only a few. So when testing a new trading method, give yourself an adequate opportunity to test it out. Carefully control your risk, so that you risk only a small percentage of your trading capital on each trade, and then, test out the new method on as many trades as possible before deciding whether or not it will work for you.

Fundamental Attribution Errors

Traders often want to build up their ego and feel good about themselves. The easiest way to do that is to take all the credit when they are successful and blame the market when they are not. This is an example of what psychologists call the *fundamental attribution error*. The fundamental attribution error is the tendency to over-attribute success to one's ability while underestimating the contributions of external circumstances. Making the fundamental attribution error too often may make you feel overly confident, and such overconfidence can be dangerous.

The fundamental attribution error is a common bias that is demonstrated by everyone at some time or other. Making such statements is normal and adaptive most of the time. It's healthy to have a positive view of yourself and view your successes as examples of your talent and ability, and sometimes, temporarily blaming external circumstances for our misfortunes is an effective coping strategy. At some point, however, one must determine exactly when an outcome is due to his or her ability and when it is due to circumstance.

It's important to realize that although skill and dedication is an essential ingredient to success, being in the right circumstance may also play a role. For example, you probably know of many times where if you could have implemented a trading strategy under the optimal market conditions, you would have made a big win. Unfortunately, those conditions didn't exist, and you didn't make a big win. Similarly, there were probably times when you made a big win, in which you could have just as easily lost had the market conditions been different.

Considering how your decisions may be influenced by the fundamental attribution error does not mean that you should underestimate your personal contribution to your trading success, but it is useful to pay attention to the tendency to underestimate the contribution of external circumstances. There are times when humility is useful. Ask yourself, "Am I taking too much credit for the success of this trade? Was I at the right place at the right time?" True self-awareness requires an objective and balanced view of your contributions. It's useful to know when your success, or failure, is the result of a factor you can control or one you cannot control.

False Consensus Effects

Suppose you decide to go long on Sears. How many other investors would agree with your decision? When people are asked such a question, they tend to overestimate the number of people who will make a similar decision. This decision-making bias is known as the *false consensus effect.*

No matter what decision you ask people to make, no matter how important the issue, and no matter what choice is made, social psychologists have demonstrated that people overestimate the number of others who will agree with them. There is a natural tendency to believe that our decisions are relatively normal and appropriate and similar to what our colleagues and peers would do in a similar situation. We use our decisions as an "anchor" and evaluate what others would do based on what we would do. This decision-making bias can contribute to feelings of over-confidence. Once we make a decision, we tend to be confident that we are correct and that others will agree with us. But they may not.

One explanation for the false consensus effect concerns how people make a decision. When making a decision regarding a ideological position, people try to piece together evidence to arrive at a decision. At some point, they organize all the information that supports one alternative over another, while discounting contradictory information. After a decision is made, evidence supporting one's decision is "available" in memory. It is easy to remember. When asked to decide how many people would make a similar decision, they still have these various pieces of confirming evidence in mind, can easily recall them, and believe that others will behave as they do based on the information they recall. Estimates of what others will do are based on inaccurate memories, rather than objective facts.

There is some evidence, however, that the tendency to make a false consensus estimate depends on how certain one is regarding a decision. Drs. Gary Marks and Norman Miller (1985), for example, manipulated the extent to which participants were certain about a decision they made. The more confidence in one's decision, the less accurate the estimate of how many others would commit to the same course of action. Thus, the more certain we are about a decision, the more we believe others will behave like us. These false consensus estimates, in turn, make us feel even more over-confident.

How do you counteract the false consensus effect? It is probably best to always be skeptical of your decisions. Consider the human tendency to seek out confirming information and make decisions based on information available in memory (availability heuristic). Making a decision is so difficult that it takes all our psychological energy to piece information together that supports our decision, but we must also look for information that refutes our decision. So after you have gathered your information, and before you draw a final conclusion, step back, and ask yourself, "Am I giving into a decision-making bias? Did I review my facts objectively or am I trying to confirm a pre-existing belief?" Always remember that your perceptions may be influenced by many common decision-making biases, such as the false consensus effect.

Resistance and Momentum

The classic boom and bust theory of the market is that a given price pattern cycle is initiated by mass mentality or perception of what future price movement will be. As traders establish their opinions (these cycles usually begin with bullish opinion) and the media reports support them, they begin to act on them, inevitably and seemingly causing their predicted pattern to develop (the boom). This confirmation of their opinions bolsters their confidence and is a source of encouragement for them to maintain their positions and to even add to them. As the predicted directional movement forms and the activity slows down, experienced traders come in and set their positions against the mass opinion. The price trend begins to change (the bust).

Logically, it would seem that this would be a good point for most people to begin liquidating their positions and taking either some profit or if they were a bit late to enter, to cut their losses short. But this is not what happens. As the price declines, investors tend to hold on, with the hopes that the price will begin rising again or that they'll have an opportunity to at least sell at the price they bought.

In general, once people are taught a certain way, and especially when they've been rewarded for their approach, they have great difficulty altering their behavior. Even if they see strong contradictory evidence, they will persist in their opinions. Successful traders who utilize momentum in their decision-making are basing their choices, at least partly, on this type of market psychology. The boom created by the mass opinion originally has a form of "inertia" as people receive affirmation about their opinions. At some point, as this momentum slows, the experienced trader realizes an opportunity of optimized probability to take advantage of the market pattern.

The resistance to alter one's behavior is what causes the trader to give back unrealized gains and, more often than not, to even take realized losses. When you're speculating or have an opinion about where the market is headed, no matter how solid you think your analysis is, it's always only good for a limited time. Recognizing this and realizing how others think and invest will give you the added edge to take advantage of opportunities to make trades with optimized probabilities.

Predictability as a Moderator of Risk Aversion

Psychologists have been studying the conditions under which people seek out risk. You may have seen a classic set of questions that has been used by psychologists to study risk:

In which stock would you prefer to invest?

(A) Stock A will produce a sure profit of $250

(B) Stock B has a 25% chance of producing a profit of $1000, but there is a 75% chance the stock will produce no profit.

About 70-80% of the people asked such questions choose option A. They prefer a sure profit of $250, even though there is a chance they can earn four times that amount by purchasing Stock B. In other words, they avoid risk when they think an investment will produce a gain.

People think differently when they consider taking a loss, however. Consider a similar question that is "framed" in terms of losses rather than profits:

In which stock would you prefer to invest?

(A) Stock A will produce a sure loss of $750

(B) Stock B has a 25% chance of losing nothing, but a 75% chance of losing $1000

When asked this question, presented in terms of losses, people tend to choose Option B. When it comes to considering a loss, they are willing to take a chance on preserving their investment. But they also accept the possibility of losing the entire investment, rather than taking a sure loss. In summary, responses to these questions show that people are risk averse when they believe they are about to make a profit, but risk seeking when they think they are on the verge of taking a loss. This is a seminal finding in investment psychology.

A recent scientific study by Drs. Lerner and Keltner reveals that this traditional understanding of risk and decision-making is not shown by everyone all of the time. One factor that predicts, or moderates, risk aversiveness is the tendency to believe that the outcomes of events, such as future stock prices, are easily predictable, in contrast to viewing outcomes as difficult to predict. In addition to measuring the tendency to view outcomes as easily predictable, Drs. Learner and Keltner asked participants to make choices similar to the ones outlined above.

They found that participants who tended to believe that outcomes are easy to predict tend to seek out risks. They are willing to take a gamble if there is a chance they can make a big win. In contrast, people who tend to believe that outcomes of events are often uncertain and difficult to predict, tend to take the sure thing. They don't like taking chances (Certainty was measured with the TANG scale of the STAXI, which is an indirect measure of certainty and predictability).

Where do you lie on this continuum? Do you tend to think that one can easily predict the future price of stocks and commodities? Do you have high expectations that prices should move in your favor? Are you often disappointed when price action is not consistent with your expectations? If you tend to agree with these questions, you may tend to seek out and take unnecessary risks. You may want to look out for this tendency. Make sure that when you make an investment, your predictions are based on solid evidence, rather than on your gut instinct. Be aware that you may tend to be a little too sure about your ability to predict events and this will make you want to take unnecessary risks.

Remember the old adage, "cut your losses short." It's probably beneficial to show caution and be appropriately risk averse. Take a sure loss, rather than take an unnecessary risk that could result in the loss of your entire investment.

Losing Found Money

Playing with the casino's or the "house's money" is considered one of the best possible situations for gamblers, and for traders, as well. Here's the situation: You place a bet and it quickly pays off. You pocket your original bet, and play with your winnings. At that point, one starts to assume one is playing with the "house's money" and not one's own. Since it's the house's money, why not be a little carefree? Why not take a little extra risk? After all, goes the thinking, if you lose, it is not really your money you are losing. But that is precisely the wrong mind-set for those who want to go home with more money than they brought. The reason is that carefully managed risk, and a healthy respect for the dangers of losing, is what drives most traders' account balances to grow. But if you believe the winnings or found money is not really your own, then what is so important about taking quick losses? What is the reason for taking only the best setups? Why bother insisting on a 3:1 risk/reward ratio? By not honoring as your own the winnings or found money you are putting at risk, you greatly increase the chances that you will not hang onto it for very long. To improve your chances of hanging on to your winnings or any form of found money, try these techniques:

Take emotional ownership: Stop thinking of the winnings or found money as anything different from your own hard-earned bucks. One way is to re-think your image of the winnings or found money: Instead of simply leaving winnings or found money in the markets, try imaging that you have taken the money out, and then put it back in. Some people actually do this kind of mental re-investing to help them view the money as theirs to keep, to invest, and to lose.

Protect it like it was your own: Stop thinking of the winnings or found money as some special fund. Treat it like any other dollar in your trading account. Do not sacrifice or give up on any of it. Fight to retain every penny of the winnings, or found money, just as you do with all the other money in your account.

Use your normal risk management techniques: On a practical level, it is useful to manage your winnings or windfall exactly the same as you manage the rest of your money. By maintaining the same risk levels, the same stop loss parameters, and the same wariness about losing, you will begin to get the same positive returns from winnings and windfall money as you do from other dollars in your trading account.

References

Bandura, A. (1977). Self-efficacy: Toward a unifying theory of behavior change. *Psychological Review, 84,* 191-215.

Barber, B., & Odean, T. (2000). Trading is hazardous to your wealth: The common stock investment performance of individual investors. *Journal of Finance, 55,* 773-806.

Cantor, N., Norem, J. K., Niedenthal, P. M., Langston, C. A., & Brower, A. M. (1987). Life tasks, self-concept, ideals, and cognitive strategies in a life transition. *Journal of Personality and Social Psychology, 53,* 1178-1191.

Chui, P. M. (2001). An experimental study of the disposition effect: Evidence from Macau. *Journal of Psychology and Financial Markets, 2,* 216-222.

Crocker, J., Sommers, S. R., & Luhtanen, R. K. (2002). Hopes dashed and dreams fulfilled: Contingencies of self-worth and graduate school admissions. *Personality and Social Psychology Bulletin, 28,* 1275-1286.

Csikszentmihalyi, M. (1997). *Finding flow.* New York: Harper Collins.

Douglas, M. (2000). *Trading in the zone: Master the market with confidence, discipline and a winning attitude.* Paramus, NJ: New York Institute of Finance.

Ellis, A. (1962). *Reason and emotion in psychotherapy.* Secaucus, NJ: Citadel.

Freud, S. (1955). Beyond the pleasure principle. In *Standard edition*. Vol. 7. London: Hogarth Press.

Gervais, S., & Odean, T. (2001). Learning to be overconfident. *Review of Financial Studies, 14,* 1-27.

Glasser, W. (1965). *Reality therapy: A new approach to psychiatry.* New York: Harper and Row.

Kiev, A. (1998). *Trading to win: The psychology of mastering the markets.* New York: John Wiley and Sons.

Lazarus, R. S. (1964). A laboratory approach to the dynamics of psychological stress. *American Psychologist, 19,* 400-411.

Lazarus, R. S. (1991). *Emotion and adaptation.* New York: Oxford University Press.

Lefevre, E. (1993). *Reminiscences of a Stock Operator.* New York: John Wiley and Sons.

Lerner, J. S., & Keltner, D. (2001). Fear, anger, and risk. *Journal of Personality and Social Psychology, 81*, 146-159.

Locke, E. A., & Latham, G. P. (2002). Building a practically useful theory of goal and task motivation: A 35-year odyssey. *American Psychologist, 57*, 705-717.

MacGregor, D. G., Slovic, P., Dreman, D., & Berry, M. (2000). Imagery, affect, and financial judgment. *Journal of Psychology and Financial Markets, 1,* 104-110.

Marks, G., & Miller, N. (1985). The effect of certainty on consensus judgments. *Personality and Social Psychology Bulletin, 11,* 165-177.

Murphy, J. J. (1999). *Technical analysis of the financial markets.* Paramus, N. J.: New York Institute of Finance.

Peale, N. V. (1952). *The power of positive thinking.* New York: Prentice Hall.

Pring, M. J. (1993). *Investment psychology explained: Classic strategies to beat the markets.* New York: John Wiley and Sons.

Radcliffe, N. M, & Klein, W. M. P. (2002). Dispositional, unrealistic and comparative optimism: Differential relations with the knowledge and processing of risk information and beliefs about risk. *Personality and Social Psychology Bulletin, 28,* 836-846.

Reilly, P. M, Sees, K. L., Shopshire, M. S., Hall, S. M, et al. (1995). Self-efficacy and illicit opioid use in a 180-day methadone detoxification treatment. *Journal of Consulting and Clinical Psychology, 63,* 158-162.

Seligman, M. E. P. (1990). *Learned optimism: How to change your mind and your life*. New York: A.A. Knopf.

Shefrin, H. (2000). *Beyond greed and fear: Understanding behavioral finance and the psychology of investing*. Boston: Harvard Business School Press.

Staw, B. M, & Ross, J. (1987). Knowing when to pull the plug. *Harvard Business Review, 65,* 68-74.

Staw, B. M, & Ross, J. (1989). Understanding behavior in escalation situations. *Science, 246,* 216-220.

Schwager, J. D. (1989). *Market wizards: Interviews with top traders.* Paramus, NJ: New York Institute of Finance.

Tharp, V. K. (1999). *Trade your way to financial freedom.* New York: McGraw-Hill.

Tversky, A. & Kaheneman, D. (1973). Availability: A heuristic for judging frequency and probability. *Cognitive Psychology, 5,* 207-232.